IMAGES
of America

COMMUNITY HOSPITAL
OF SAN BERNARDINO

This ambulance might have been used at Ramona Hospital, the forerunner of Community Hospital of San Bernardino. Ramona Hospital was a two-story building with no elevators. Patients had to be carried by hand on a gurney. The ambulance team usually consisted of one tall man and one short man. On the way up the stairs, the short man went first, while on the way down the tall man was first.

ON THE COVER: Santa hears the hopes and dreams of a little patient at Community Hospital. She is no doubt wishing for a less scratchy throat, the return of her tonsils, or some ice cream. Santa visited the Children's Ward each year to spread a little good cheer to anyone filling a bed at Christmas time. (Courtesy California Room, Feldheym Central Library.)

IMAGES
of America

COMMUNITY HOSPITAL
OF SAN BERNARDINO

Joyce A. Hanson,
Suzie Earp, and Erin Shanks

ARCADIA
PUBLISHING

Published by Arcadia Publishing
Charleston SC, Chicago IL, Portsmouth NH, San Francisco CA

Printed in the United States of America

Library of Congress Control Number: 2009922892

For all general information contact Arcadia Publishing at:
Telephone 843-853-2070
Fax 843-853-0044
E-mail sales@arcadiapublishing.com
For customer service and orders:
Toll-Free 1-888-313-2665

Visit us on the Internet at www.arcadiapublishing.com

This book is dedicated to all the wonderful people at Community Hospital, past, present, and future, and the community they serve.

CONTENTS

ACKNOWLEDGMENTS

Thank you to my wonderful coauthors. Suzie Earp is a super caption writer, and Erin Shanks can scan anyone under the table. Without their hard work and dedication, this book would not have been possible. Thank you as well to my friends and top-notch rewrite team at Community Hospital: Tobey Robertson, director of marketing and communications, and especially Kimiko Ford, vice president of mission services. We spent many long hours together working on this manuscript. Because of her commitment and insights, the manuscript was vastly improved. A special thank-you goes to Jack Brown for generously sharing his memories and photographs of the Sammy Davis Jr. gala. Thank you as well to the knowledgeable and very helpful folks at the California Room of the Feldheym Library. All of you rock! All images used in this book come from the collections at Community Hospital unless otherwise noted.

INTRODUCTION

At the dawn of the 20th century, 6,150 people, about 50 saloons, several hotels, numerous stores, a red-light vice district, and pleasant residential areas called San Bernardino, California, home. The city had grown substantially since being founded by the Mormons in 1851; at least some of this growth can be attributed to its geographic location. San Bernardino was located in an area generally considered to be ideal for general health and a recuperative place for those respiratory conditions. But despite its reputation as a "healthy" place, most health care was delivered in private homes, and it wasn't until the late 1860s that a "health care facility" was established in the city; even that was merely a place that primarily treated those with smallpox. Finally, in 1886, the county Board of Supervisors authorized San Bernardino's first official hospital, the San Bernardino County Charity Hospital. As its name suggests, the county hospital treated those unable to pay for private medical services. Non-charity cases still relied on private medical care.

Dr. George B. Rowell was one of the physicians who had established a successful medical practice by 1900, and he wanted a certified medical graduate to share his practice with him. Dr. Rowell believed that his best chance to find someone with a formal medical education was to look to England, where medical licensing was well established, unlike the United States. In 1902, Dr. Rowell placed an advertisement for a medical partner in the *London Times*. A 30-year-old graduate of the Edinburgh University Medical School and London's famed St. Thomas Hospital, Dr. Henry William Mills, answered Rowell's advertisement. At the time, Dr. Mills was a fellow in the Royal College of Surgeons and the Royal College of Physicians. The history of Community Hospital begins with Dr. Mills's arrival in San Bernardino in February 1903. Soon after arriving, Dr. Mills realized that the surgical facilities available were woefully inadequate. Mills was determined to correct this and in 1906 converted an old wooden residence at the corner of Fourth and F Streets into the Marlborough Hospital. Dr. Mills along with Dr. M. Campbell Billings operated the facility until the need for additional space became acute in 1909.

Dr. Mills approached his friend the distinguished attorney Ralph Swing for funding to purchase land at the site of an old adobe saloon located at the corner of Fourth Street and Arrowhead Avenue. After much discussion, in March 1909, Swing and Mills invested $10,000, purchased the land, and began construction of a two-story stucco hospital building with beds for 42 patients and an adequate operating room. Ramona Hospital opened its doors in February 1910. Ralph Swing became the first business advisor, and Dr. Mills was the hospital administrator. Between 1910 and 1931, Ramona Hospital was the only first-class surgical hospital in the San Bernardino area. During World War I, Ramona Hospital took care of numerous victims of the devastating influenza epidemic that swept the country and army camps. After World War I, as community needs grew, Ramona Hospital expanded, adding a nurse's training school and living quarters. About 1920, Dr. Mills founded a second hospital, Sequoia, in a two-story residence at the southeast corner of Fifth and D Streets. Drs. Clause Lashlee, Russell W. Prince, and C. C. Owen, now historical figures in the medical history of San Bernardino, became associated with Dr. Mills. Dr. Mills died on March 26, 1927, at the age of 54 from septicemia, an infection of the bloodstream. Despite Dr. Mills's early death, Ramona Hospital continued operating under the administration of Dr. Claude H. Lashlee, but the Great Depression took its toll on the hospital. In 1932, the bank took over the operation of the hospital, which had been held as a proprietary institution. It seemed as if Ramona Hospital would close its doors forever.

Dr. Lashlee, along with 15 other doctors, a dentist, and one layman, immediately formed the Ramona Hospital Association, donating and raising $40,014 to buy Ramona Hospital back from the bank and keep the doors open. The group then went ahead and added an additional 23-bed surgical wing, increasing the hospital to a 65-bed capacity. Despite their optimism, times were still hard and money was tight. To keep the doors open, the 18 members of the association made monthly donations to the hospital so that it could pay salaries, utilities, and operating expenses. Within four years, it became apparent that even with careful management the association could not manage to meet expenses and pay property taxes. To alleviate this problem, in 1938, the Ramona Hospital Association reorganized itself into a charitable nonprofit corporation with a new name—San Bernardino Community Hospital.

Slowly but surely, San Bernardino Community Hospital began paying its bills on time and even managed to buy some additional property to the north and east of the hospital. It was in March 1943 that Virginia Henderson, the woman who would play a major role in the hospital's expansion, began working as office manager. Henderson would work her way up in the administration and become the hospital's administrator, one of the few women hospital administrators in the country who was not affiliated with a religious order. Despite shortages of essential medical supplies, under Henderson's guidance, San Bernardino Community Hospital gained status as an accredited hospital by the Joint Commission on Hospital Administration.

After agreeing to sell the property at Fourth Street and Arrowhead Avenue to the City of San Bernardino for the construction of a civic center, San Bernardino Community Hospital began its search for a new home. In April 1953, the newly reorganized Board of Directors purchased land at Seventeenth Street and Western Avenue, hiring the firm of Buttress and McClellan to determine if the community could support a 200-bed hospital. Frustration followed as the hospital tried to secure financing to construct the new building. Turned down by a major life insurance company and the federal Reconstruction Finance Corporation, and told it would be 73rd on a list of Southern California hospitals seeking state funding, Drs. Eugene Hull, Emmett Tisinger, and Delbert Williams continued to search for financing. Finally Massachusetts Life Insurance Company committed to a half-million-dollar loan but only after completion. Citizen's National Bank and the American National Bank eventually provided interim financing for the building project. The new hospital could be built, but it had no money for furnishings. Between late 1956 and 1957, San Bernardino Community Hospital joined forces with St. Bernardine's to launch a public drive for funds called the United Appeal for Hospital Beds. The public campaign raised about $850,000, but Community Hospital still needed about $150,000. The new hospital at Seventeenth Street and Western Avenue was completed in April 1958. It was the first completely air-conditioned hospital in the city. It had 133 beds, 30 bassinets, 275 employees, and a shortage of furnishings.

In 1954, entertainer Sammy Davis Jr. had been critically injured in a car accident and taken to San Bernardino Community Hospital for treatment. It was the surgical skill of Dr. Frederick H. Hull that saved Davis's sight in his right eye. As a thank-you, Davis organized and presented a star-studded benefit show for the hospital on Sunday evening, November 15, 1958. Over 8,000 people attended the gala, held at the Swing Auditorium at the National Orange Show and featuring Judy Garland, Tina Louise, Shirley MacLaine, Diane Carroll, and many others. The show raised over $31,048 for additional hospital furnishings.

In the 1960s and 1970s, the hospital continued to expand and modernize. Only three years after moving to the new location, a major expansion program added 95 beds, conference rooms, an auditorium, enlarged emergency facilities, a new obstetrical delivery area, and a service building. In 1964, San Bernardino Community Hospital added a new laboratory and, in 1967, a new lobby and business office. The year 1969 saw more expansion: a 125-bed extended-care facility, a new physical therapy building, the expansion of the maternity wing, and renovation of the wing used for intensive care and coronary care. The radiology department, cardiopulmonary, and central supply were enlarged as well, and by 1971, the extended-care beds were converted to acute care, bringing the total bed count to 322. Three hundred and six medical personnel and 1,150 employees provided the best medical care to the patients.

As the surrounding area continued to grow, so did the hospital. When the facility could no longer accommodate demand for services, Community Hospital began looking for a new location. In 1980, ten sites in three areas were being considered: San Bernardino, Rialto, and Colton. The board carefully considered all sites, eventually deciding on relocation to Rialto. Controversy ensued. The city council, backed by Mayor Bob Holcomb, unanimously voted to oppose the move. A movement to oust the 18-member board of directors followed, and eventually 12 of the 18 were removed. Meanwhile 600 employees lent their names to an advertisement supporting the move. After two years of contention, the new board of directors decided to remain in San Bernardino, citing economic considerations. Between 1986 and 1988, the San Bernardino Community Hospital Foundation conducted a fund-raising campaign to raise $2.2 million for the new facility. About 800 employees, physicians, board and corporate members, the auxiliary, community businesses and individuals, corporations, and foundations pledged and contributed $2.3 million. The largest gift was a $1 million plus contribution from Monida B. Cummings. Cummings was the daughter of John Moses Browning, who designed and fashioned the breech mechanism for rifles, patenting the famous Winchester rifle in 1879. In December 1989, a new five-story, 150,000-square-foot tower named for Monida Cummings opened on Medical Center Drive. This new hospital housed patient rooms, a larger emergency center, highly advanced diagnostic imaging, a cardiopulmonary center, new bigger cafeteria, and state-of-the-art intensive care and coronary care units.

Since that time, Community Hospital has continued to grow and serve the community. In 1993, the $15 million, 60-bed Robert H. Ballard Rehabilitation Hospital opened. At the time, it was the only hospital specializing in comprehensive physical rehabilitation in San Bernardino, Riverside, Mono, and Inyo Counties. In 1996, a 57,000-square-foot, three-level medical office building was constructed and connected to the hospital by a bridge that spans Medical Center Drive. Today Community Hospital stands as a 321-bed, nonprofit hospital with more than 1,000 employees. Community Hospital affiliated with Catholic Healthcare West in 1998, although the hospital remains non-denominational. The employees, medical staff, and volunteers are known for living the Catholic Healthcare West mission every day in the work they do to care for the community. The mission statement says it all: "We dedicate our resources to delivering compassionate, high quality, affordable health services; serving and advocating for our sisters and brothers who are poor and disenfranchised; and partnering with others in the community to improve the quality of life."

Recently Community Hospital received the prestigious UNICEF/WHO "Baby Friendly" designation, one of only 61 "Baby Friendly" hospitals in the United States. Community Hospital is also known for its outstanding obstetrics program, called Babies First, guiding mothers-to-be and their families through every step of prenatal care, delivery, and post-delivery. Community Hospital is proud to be a trusted resource of community health services and educational support for the region.

Virginia Henderson was the Community Hospital administrator for many years. She began at the old Ramona Hospital in 1943, working her way up to administrator, an unusual accomplishment for a woman at the time. Many people who worked at the hospital said it was because of Virginia that they stayed, including doctors, nurses, and staff. Not a single negative word has ever been uttered about Virginia by the employees.

One

THE EARLY YEARS

Dr. George Rowell (right) came from Canada to San Bernardino and established a successful medical practice in the late 19th century. Dr. Rowell wanted someone to share his practice, but he was looking for a certified medical graduate who had some experience. Rowell looked to England, where medical licensing was well established. Dr. Henry W. Mills answered Rowell's advertisement and was hired. Mills would become the founding father of Community Hospital.

Dr. Henry Mills was the founder of Ramona Hospital, later renamed Community Hospital. He was a graduate of Edinborough University Medical School and London's famed St. Thomas Hospital. In 1909, he convinced his good friend Ralph Swing to invest $10,000 to buy the property at Fourth Street and Arrowhead Avenue. One year later on February 2, 1910, Ramona Hospital opened its doors. The hospital included a first-class surgical unit and was the only private hospital available until 1931, when St. Bernardine's opened its doors. Mills, a self-proclaimed "belly surgeon" famous for his post-operative castor oil highballs—a mixture of castor oil and root beer—also began a nurses training program and established another hospital, the Sequoia, at Fifth and D Streets. Tragically, Dr. Mills died at the age of 54 from a tooth infection resulting in septicemia. The first antibiotics that could have saved Dr. Mills's life were not developed until the 1930s.

Ralph Swing became Dr. Henry Mill's business partner. In 1903, Dr. Mills successfully delivered Swing's first child in San Bernardino. The child's name was Everett Swing. Ralph Swing was a young local attorney in 1903 and then went on to be on the Board of Water Commissioners for the City of San Bernardino, the president of the San Bernardino Valley Centennial Celebration in 1910, and state senator for many years. When Dr. Mills wanted to purchase a building at Fourth Street and Arrowhead Avenue to build a professional hospital, he approached Ralph Swing to invest. The Swing family remained strongly involved with Community Hospital throughout their lives.

Ramona Hospital was located on the corner of Fourth Street and Arrowhead Avenue. Built in 1910, it was the forerunner of Community Hospital. The location was chosen because of its proximity to trolley stops and its lush, green, soothing views of the verdant valley. Before 1910, San Bernardino had a county hospital for infectious disease only and Dr. Mills operated out of a two-story home at Fourth and F Streets. Through the joint efforts of Dr. Henry Mills and attorney Ralph Swing, a first-class, professional, 42-bed private hospital was built on the corner where an old adobe saloon once stood. (Courtesy Steven Shaw.)

This advertisement for the Ramona Hospital was printed in the *Evening Index* during a special section celebrating the San Bernardino Valley Centennial in 1910. Ramona Hospital accepted no consumptive cases and boasted of operating rooms, a department of obstetrics, a pathology lab, and an "elaborate X-ray plant." While reasonable rates may have attracted many patients, it was the excellent care they received from physicians and nursing staff that kept patients coming back. Professional medical care in San Bernardino was just being instituted at the turn of the 20th century. Ramona Hospital set the standard for future medical service. This hospital was in continual use until a new facility was built in 1958. (Courtesy California Room, Feldheym Central Library.)

These are original bills from Ramona Hospital. In 1915, an eight-day stay including anesthesia and surgical dressings cost Mrs. S. E. Andrews $26.20. But something wasn't right—after being discharged on September 3, Andrews returned for another two-day stay, adding $9.70 to her medical expenses. It is too bad these original hospital invoices cannot explain why Andrews returned. Between 1910 and 1931, Ramona Hospital was the only first-class surgical hospital in the San Bernardino area. During World War I, Ramona Hospital took care of numerous victims of the devastating influenza epidemic that swept the country and army camps. After World War I, as community needs grew, Ramona Hospital expanded, adding a nurse's training school and living quarters.

In March 1918, Dr. Mills was commissioned as a captain in the Army Medical Corps. By July, he was working in Base Hospital No. 35 at Savenay, France, where he was decorated for his work with the wounded. When the war ended in November 1918, he was transferred to Liverpool, England. He returned to San Bernardino in April 1919 and lost no time in returning to his medical practice. Drs. Claude Lashlee, Russell W. Prince, and C. C. Owen, now historical figures in the medical history of San Bernardino, became associated with Dr. Mills. Dr. Mills died on March 26, 1927, at the age of 54 from septicemia, an infection of the bloodstream. Despite Dr. Mills's early death, Ramona Hospital continued operating under the administration of Dr. Claude H. Lashlee. (Courtesy San Bernardino Pioneer and Historical Society.)

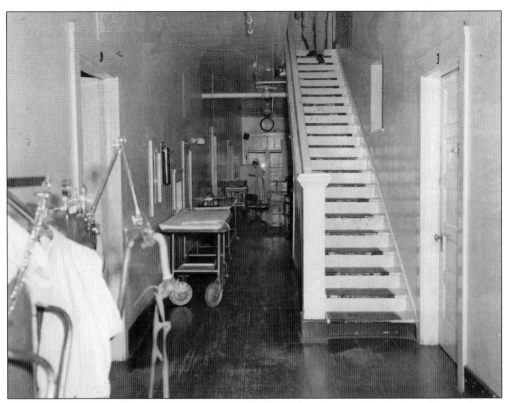

The photograph above is the street entrance of the old Ramona Hospital at Fourth Street and Arrowhead Avenue. One of the most often quoted memories from patients and physicians alike was the lack of elevators in a hospital that had labor rooms on the first floor and delivery rooms on the second. Likewise, surgical patients always remembered the weather on the day of their surgery. The entrance to surgery was not accessible through the main hospital. Patients were transported outside and then into surgery. The photograph at left shows the rear entrance to the building. Dr. George Spelman remembered, "The hospital itself was a wooden structure. I remember in the '50's, I generally drove around to the lower part and parked my car. One day an earthquake occurred just as I was leaving my car and moving towards that long flight of stairs to go in that entrance. The building was just flexing and shaking, almost like it was doing a Rumba."

Here is a rare photograph of a patient room at Ramona Hospital. Patients needed a degree of tolerance; no air-conditioning meant hot rooms during the summer on the upper floors, where the patient rooms were located, and in the screened porches, which served as wards. According to Dr. Breck Petersen, there was one surgical suite and only one dressing room serving doctors and nurses, requiring close cooperation between them.

The hospital maintained a training school for nurses in connection with its work. The nurse in training was given a complete course of lectures and trained in all branches of the profession by the doctors at Ramona. Estelle Corbitt, a San Bernardino native, was matron when the hospital opened in 1910. Nurses included Dena Brown, Ruth Williams, Ruth Andelstedt, and Kate Schamalhofer, all of San Bernardino.

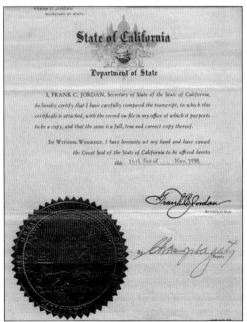

With the Great Depression and increasing taxes threatening the survival of Ramona Hospital, the bank took ownership. Dr. Lashlee, 15 other doctors, a dentist, and one layman formed the Ramona Hospital Association, donating and raising over $40,000 to keep the doors open. The group then added an additional 23-bed surgical wing, increasing the hospital's capacity to 65 beds. Despite their optimism, times were still hard and money was tight. Within four years, it became apparent that even with careful management, the association could not manage to meet expenses and pay the hospital's property taxes. To alleviate this problem, in 1938, the Ramona Hospital Association reorganized itself into a charitable nonprofit corporation with a new name—San Bernardino Community Hospital. Drs. Eugene Hull, Arthur Varden, J. N. Baylis, Claude Lashlee, and F. M. Gardner signed incorporation papers, pictured at left.

The facilities at the old hospital at Fourth Street and Arrowhead Avenue were not the most modern, but the food was always made with care. Here Myrtle Clark cooks breakfast for the patients and staff while Drs. D. B. Williams (rear) and J. N. Martin (front) look on. This photograph was taken in 1957 just before the move to the new modern facility on Seventeenth Street and Western Avenue.

This photograph was taken on the last day of the year in 1957 at Ramona Hospital. Clearly office space was cramped there. In the photograph are, from left to right, Marjorie Oltman, Beverly Oliver, Mildred Klan, Thelma Bryant, and Roberta Massey. The new hospital that opened the following year had a lot more space for these duties, and these ladies no longer had to share desks.

The entire building was fully equipped with an electric bell system for the use of patients; also a system of speaking tubes connected the office with all parts of the building. According to literature at the time, "This splendid institution is architecturally so beautiful, so finely equipped and so capably managed that the sick and distressed who come within its walls find a new inspiration and desire to live." In 1910, the city of San Bernardino had about 10,000 residents. Ramona Hospital was designed to take advantage of the beautiful environment with views of the local mountains. The balconies permitted patients on the second floor to get out in the air while convalescing. (Courtesy California Room, Feldheym Central Library.)

Two

A New Hospital

By the early 1950s, it was apparent that the old facility was no longer adequate. Hospital administrator Virginia Henderson was credited for gaining the community's support and the board's approval to establish a building committee and raise the funds to relocate the hospital. Here Henderson and Dr. Emmett Tisinger oversee the survey crew as they lay out the new 133-bed hospital at Seventeenth Street and Western Avenue in February 1957.

Several of the doctors who served Community Hospital were at the ground-breaking ceremony in 1957. They were happy to welcome a new facility yet at the same time expressed nostalgia for the family-like atmosphere of the old Ramona Hospital. In the words of Dr. Petersen, Ramona Hospital "worked because it was a community." From left to right are Drs. J. N. Martin, W. E. Freeman, E. H. Hull, and Steve Rebwald.

Hospital administrator Virginia Henderson turns the first shovel of soil for the construction of the new state-of-the-art hospital that would supply medical care for the citizens of San Bernardino and surrounding areas. The hospital was built for a cost of $1.5 million and completed in April 1958. With Henderson are an unidentified RN and Dr. Delbert Williams, who served on the original building committee for the hospital.

Virginia Henderson toured many hospitals to gain insight into construction design before the plans were developed. A relatively new, cost-effective construction method called tilt-up was used to build the new hospital. The concrete panels were formed and poured on the ground, allowed to dry sufficiently and then tilted up into position by cranes. The walls were then braced in place, and when all the walls were up, they were connected at the corners and the roof.

The new hospital began construction in March 1957 and was completed in April 1958. This one-story facility contained a total of 58,374 square feet. It was designed so that two additional wings could be added without altering original specifications. Directors of the hospital thought it wise to plan far into the future in regards to the number of beds, said Warren Freeman, chairman of the lay advisory committee.

The clean lines and unpretentious facade of the new Community Hospital embodied the efficient design, which successfully transitioned the team of doctors, nurses, staff, and patients to the new site. Despite the doctors' misgivings about changing locations, the new sense of openness and space was highly valued. The new hospital could accommodate twice the number of patients.

A few members of the original building committee line up for their picture on dedication day in April 1958. From left to right are Dr. J. Needham Martin; Dr. Emmett L. Tisinger, who resigned because of ill health at an earlier date; Clinton H. Smith (of Portland Cement); Dr. Delbert Williams; and Dr. William H. Wilson. Not pictured are Dr. E. H. Hull, chairman of the committee, and B. W. Vaughn.

Moving day came at long last. Moving a whole hospital was a formidable task, but Virginia Henderson had it planned from the bulkiest of equipment down to the tiniest of patients. The move went smoothly with plenty of help from staff and volunteers alike. Allied Van Lines volunteered their entire fleet to transport the patients. The one thing that doctors insisted upon was that every van would have a doctor to be with the patients. Dr. George Spelman remembered making three trips in the vans with patients. When patients got to the hospital, they were quickly settled in their new rooms. Long lines of vans and trucks pulled into the new Community Hospital at regular intervals to dispatch their loads to waiting hands.

The nurses and staff who helped make the move from the Ramona Hospital to the new Community Hospital location pose for this historic first day at the new facility in 1958. They are, from left to right, RN Eileen Semonite, RN Mary Dennis, RN Lena Myhre, RN Ester Wilson, RN Leta Bossard, RN Lois Basket, nurse's aide Nellie Belt, unknown, hospital administrator Virginia Henderson, Lila Barhurst, June Simmons, and Dorothy DeMuth.

A limousine was rented to move the tiniest patients from the Ramona Hospital to the new facility in 1958. The registered nurses who helped with this precious cargo were Leta Bossard (left) and Helen Cash (right). Everything went smoothly the day of the big move, and not a single patient was lost, nor any equipment either.

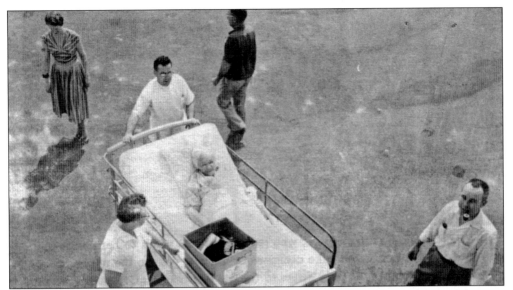

An elderly patient gets plenty of attention on the day Community Hospital moved from its downtown location to Seventeenth Street and Western Avenue. Virginia Henderson (left rear) planned and organized the move, which was executed flawlessly. Also seen in this photograph are Phil Shelly, Claris Jackson, and board member Warren E. Freeman (right front).

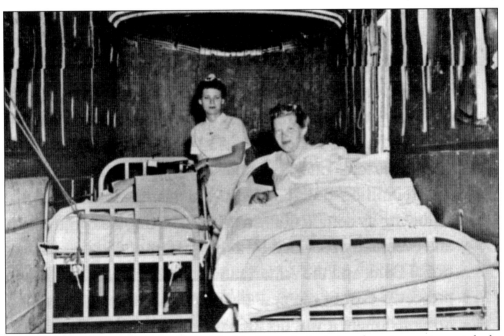

When the new hospital was finally finished in 1958, the logistics of moving equipment, beds, patients, and supplies fell to Virginia Henderson. Every member of the staff pitched in to help make the move a success. Local moving companies offered their huge vans to move beds and even some patients to the new location. Pictured here, nurse Genevieve Bozick attends patients who were moved, bed and all, on moving day.

The newly completed Community Hospital created a stir around the world for community hospital buildings. In 1959, *Modern Health Care* named Community "Hospital of the Month" for its efficient design. In this photograph, representatives from the Peninsula Community Hospital building committee came to check out the new San Bernardino hospital and speak to Virginia Henderson (seated), administrator of Community Hospital. (Courtesy California Room, Feldheym Central Library.)

In 1957, Community Hospital applied for and was granted accreditation by the joint commission on hospital accreditation founded by the American Medical Association. This was equivalent to the Good Housekeeping "Seal of Approval" and told the public that this hospital was a good place to get care. The newly accredited Community Hospital opened the doors to its new location in April 1958.

The old and new facilities at Community Hospital are pictured here; on the left is the entrance of the Ramona Hospital at Fourth Street and Arrowhead Avenue, where the hallways were crowded with equipment and the physicians had to run up and down the stairs to care for the patients. On the right is the hallway of the sleek, uncluttered facilities of the new hospital, with room for patients and equipment.

The kitchen in the new hospital was a huge improvement over the cramped quarters at the Ramona Hospital. The hospital took care of all the special diet needs of patients and employees alike. Everything was made on-site, including all the baking of bread and pastries. Large commercial ovens and a thoroughly modern kitchen made this all possible when the new hospital was completed in 1958.

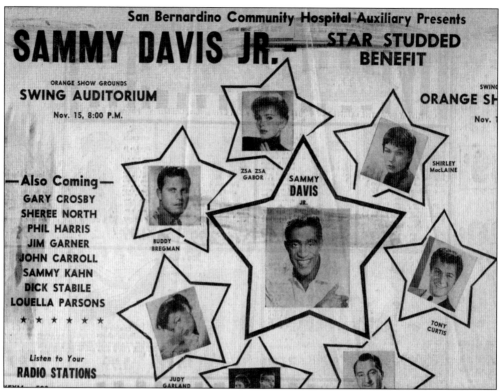

San Bernardino Community Hospital Auxiliary Presents

SAMMY DAVIS JR. — STAR STUDDED BENEFIT

ORANGE SHOW GROUNDS
SWING AUDITORIUM

Nov. 15, 8:00 P.M.

SWING
ORANGE SH

Nov. 1

—Also Coming—
GARY CROSBY
SHEREE NORTH
PHIL HARRIS
JIM GARNER
JOHN CARROLL
SAMMY KAHN
DICK STABILE
LOUELLA PARSONS

★ ★ ★ ★ ★

Listen to Your
RADIO STATIONS

ZSA ZSA GABOR

SAMMY **DAVIS** JR.

SHIRLEY MacLAINE

BUDDY BREGMAN

TONY CURTIS

JUDY GARLAND

COMMUNITY HOSPITAL
SAN BERNARDINO, CALIFORNIA

The San Bernardino Community Hospital Auxiliary cordially invites you to be a patron and patroness of the Sammy Davis, Jr. Benefit featuring prominent artists of stage, screen and television on Saturday evening, November 15, 1958, 8 o'clock Swing Auditorium, National Orange Show. These special seats, which include a reception honoring the artists, are limited and may be accepted until October 15, 1958.

All proceeds are for needed hospital equipment. Minimum donation $25.00 per couple.

Make checks payable to Community Hospital Auxiliary Benefit.

Mail in enclosed envelope to Mrs. Lloyd Griffith 3508 Broadmoor Boulevard San Bernardino.

On November 19, 1954, Sammy Davis Jr. was in a serious automobile accident on Kendall Drive in San Bernardino. He was admitted to the old hospital at Fourth Street and Arrowhead Avenue with multiple injuries, including serious damage to his eyes. Although Davis lost his left eye, Dr. Frederick Hull was able to save the sight in the other. Sammy Davis Jr. came back to San Bernardino to raise funds for the new hospital, and he convinced many of the biggest stars of the era to join him. Besides those stars listed on this flyer, Danny Thomas, Zsa Zsa Gabor, Shirley MacLaine, Sydney Poitier, and Judy Garland joined in the fun. The evening was a night to remember as the sold-out crowd of 8,000 packed into Swing Auditorium on November 15, 1958, to witness a show like no other.

The ushers for the gala evening were members of the fraternity Beta Tau Omega at Valley College. Jack Brown, now chairman and CEO of Stater Brothers Markets, was then the president of the fraternity. Jack vividly remembers the evening with the stars. From left to right are Don Leaned, Jack Brown, Sammy Davis Jr., and Jim Fuller at the reception after the show. (Courtesy Jack Brown.)

An exclusive after-event party at the Arrowhead Springs Hotel was planned, and Dr. Hull saw that all the boys in the fraternity were invited to thank them for their service. The members were all allowed to bring dates and danced and mixed with the stars who had performed at the gala. Jack Brown is at left center. (Courtesy Jack Brown.)

In these photographs, Dr. Fred Hull and Sammy Davis Jr. enjoy a jam session. Sammy Davis Jr. remained good friends with Dr. Hull and his family through the years following the car accident in San Bernardino. Dr. Hull remembered that Davis "was very kind to the family." At one time, Dr. Hull's daughter and her boyfriend went to see a play in New York City that Davis was in and she wanted to go backstage and see Sammy. Although her boyfriend doubted they could go backstage to see him, Davis cleared his dressing room and gave the young couple about 20 minutes of one-on-one time. Sammy Davis Jr. always credited Dr. Hull with saving his eyesight after the accident and remained grateful for the care he received at Community Hospital.

This photograph shows Dr. Fred Hull and Sammy Davis Jr. fooling around with a photo opportunity. That Sammy Davis Jr. could see well enough to take a photograph was considered a miracle of sorts following a car accident on Kendall Drive. Sammy Davis Jr. was taken to Community Hospital, and Dr. Hull was the surgeon who saved Davis's eyesight that day, beginning a friendship that lasted a lifetime.

RETURNS FAVOR—Entertainer Sammy Davis, Jr. receives scroll in appreciation for his help to San Bernardino Community Hospital in putting on three-hour benefit. Making the presentation are Dr. J. Needham Martin, hospital board president and Mrs. Virginia Henderson, administrator.

Pleased Patient Performs In Hospital Benefit Show

The return of a grateful patient to San Bernardino Community Hospital made news last month.

Pleased with the care he received there when he was involved in a near-fatal accident four years ago, versatile entertainer Sammy Davis, Jr. promised hospital officials he would help with their program to build and equip a new facility.

BIGGEST EVER

They put on the biggest benefit show ever held in San Bernardino, according to hospital administrator Virginia Henderson.

"It was the first time in history that the Orange Show auditorium was filled to capacity," Mrs. Henderson said.

Davis made good his promise, and brought with him a galaxy of famous Hollywood stars.

SPECTACULAR

Nearly 8,000 people paid more than $31,000 to see the spectacular entertainment.

The record-breaking crowd not only enjoyed impersonations, singing and dancing by grateful patient Davis, but was treated to acts by Judy Garland, Danny Thomas, actress Shirley MacLaine, and other stars during the three-hour performance.

Delighted with results of the show, Mrs. Henderson announced that the money will be used to purchase new equipment for the hospital.

During the evening, Davis was presented with a scroll in appreciation for his help to the community hospital.

Sammy Davis Jr. became an important figure in Community Hospital's history. In 1958, he put together a star-studded fund-raiser for Community Hospital for needed hospital equipment. The benefit raised $31,048 and was the highlight of the entertainment season in San Bernardino. In this photograph, Dr. J. Needham Martin, president of the Board of Directors, and Virginia Henderson, hospital administrator, thank Davis for his support.

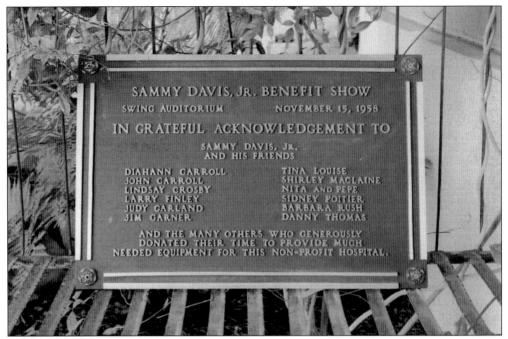

A bronze plaque pays tribute to Sammy Davis Jr. and all of the performers who came to the Swing Auditorium in November 1958 to raise money for equipment and supplies for the hospital. If not for their generous support, Community Hospital would have struggled to equip the new facility at Seventeenth Street and Western Avenue.

This shows the evolution of the Community Hospital. At left is the old hospital at Fourth Street and Arrowhead Avenue, the center photograph is the new hospital at Seventeenth Street and Western Avenue, and the photograph at right is after the addition in 1964 of a new lobby and entrance. Community Hospital has constantly grown over its 100-year history, adding services and beds as the community has needed.

Three

OUR PEOPLE

The "top brass" at Community Hospital in 1960 included, from left to right, administrator Virginia Henderson; Barbara Lunceford, president of the auxiliary; and Fern Warren, head nurse. Due to the doctors' concern about having volunteers at a patient's bedside, these three women took their responsibility for training the 140 incoming volunteers very seriously, making sure they followed protocol of the group, including dress codes and adherence to the Volunteer Pledge.

Folding surgical linen supplies are, from left to right, registered nurse Fern Warren, Gail Harrison, Mrs. Drake, Barbara Lunceford, and Mrs. Schulze. This is a good example of how the auxiliary and nurses worked hand in hand on projects. The linens were folded by the professionals but placed in storage cabinets by the volunteers. Nurse Warren oversees the entire procedure to ensure the linens are folded correctly for surgical use.

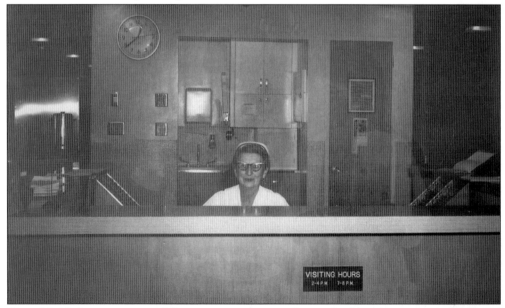

Nurse Ida Nielson sits at one of the nursing stations in the new building, supervising the flow of visitors and patient care. The innovative design made nursing staff easily accessible to families, doctors, and other staff. This was in stark contrast to the crowded, cramped conditions at the old hospital. (Courtesy California Room, Feldheym Central Library.)

Teddy Weeks, RN, was head nurse on Wing 400 for many years, participating in many in-service training measures to ensure a smooth running facility. Weeks later became director of Volunteer Services. Weeks is the first of three generations of the Weeks family to work at Community Hospital: her daughter-in-law Patti Weeks, RN, joined the hospital as a clerk in 1966, and grandson Jonathan later joined the clinical laboratory team.

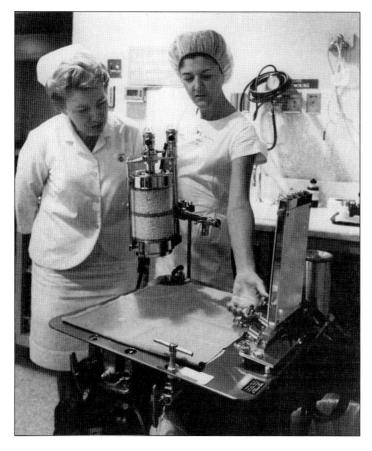

The opening of the hospital in 1958 allowed room for all the demands of the new electronic equipment quickly making its way into everyday diagnostic care that had been previously unavailable at Community Hospital. In this photograph, the OR staff proudly displays its state-of-the-art equipment. Hospital administrators from as far away as Denmark came to tour the hospital when it opened.

Children are special at Community Hospital. A reassuring environment with quality care for younger patients, the pediatric unit provides services for children from newborn to age 13. Here a nurse checks on a young patient. Community Hospital's team of experts is committed to provide the finest in personalized medical care and to make the hospital stay a positive and warm experience for the young patients.

Department of the month: Obstetrics
Days in former Ramona Hospital are recalled

"Mother Moe" Marquess left, and Delta Garrison check on a piece of equipment in O.B.

Hazel Johnston at one of the incubators in the Nursery.

Magdalena Ortiz checks the sterilizer in O.B.

The well-being of mothers and babies has always been a primary concern. The new facility was certainly much expanded, with three labor rooms and two delivery rooms. In 1960, another expansion added three delivery rooms, eight labor rooms, and 36 bassinets. In 1971, an entire wing was dedicated to labor and delivery. New equipment such as incubators, sterilizers, and bilirubin lights were also added.

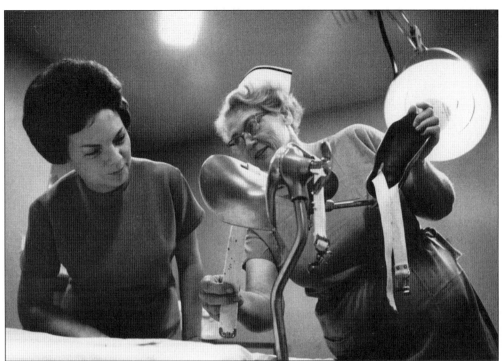

Ongoing training with the latest equipment and technology was a hallmark of Community Hospital, along with educational opportunities to strengthen staff skills. Seen here is Maxine Mitchell (left) getting a lesson from RN Doris Moseley. "Mo" as she was affectionately known, managed the obstetrical ward with full authority. Doctors, nurses, and patients alike all loved Mo dearly. She was an excellent nurse with an instinct for obstetrics. (Courtesy California Room, Feldheym Central Library.)

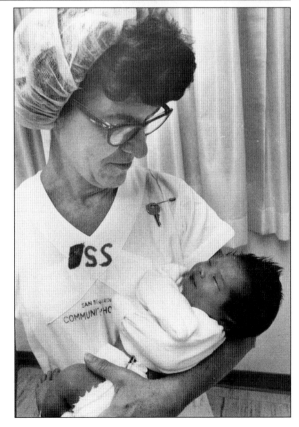

Community Hospital has long been known as the place to have babies in the valley and surrounding areas. The maternity ward was kept hopping during the baby boom years, and in 1970, the hospital delivered 2,232 babies. Florence Emminger, RN, holds a newborn. Florence went on to be recognized by *Who's Who in American Women* for outstanding achievement in her field. (Courtesy California Room, Feldheym Central Library.)

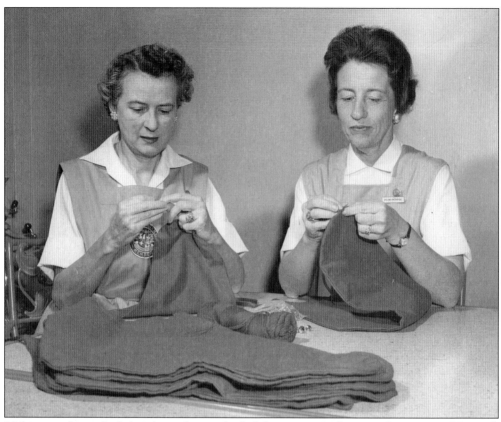

Making stockings for babies born during the holidays was a tradition at Community Hospital. Members of the auxiliary made dozens of Christmas stockings during the holidays, and each newborn was sent home in their very own stocking. Pictured in this photograph are two of Santa's helpers, volunteers Elizabeth Hiles (left) and Velma Monroe (right).

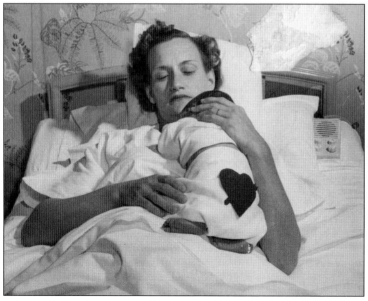

And the fun didn't stop at Christmas. The auxiliary worked to make all the holidays bright by making special remembrances for each new arrival. Even Valentine's Day was celebrated with specially decorated heart attire for the youngest of patients. In this photograph, Mrs. E. Verner holds her new little bundle of joy.

Here three-and-a-half-year-old patient Matthew Cabot recovers successfully in the new improved Pediatric Unit with his nurse Jean Melchoir at the new hospital at Seventeenth Street and Western Avenue. Creating a child-friendly environment with clowns on the walls made a scary experience more comforting for a young patient. (Courtesy California Room, Feldheym Central Library.)

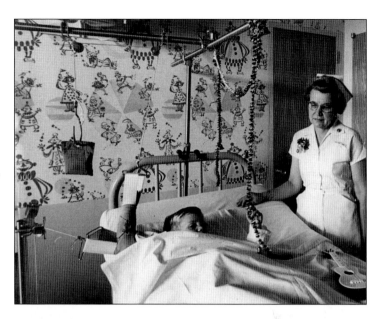

Longtime registered nurse at Community Hospital Mary Neill couldn't be happier with the facilities at the new hospital, but knowing that Community Hospital appreciated her excellent nursing skills was more important. The longevity of Community Hospital's nursing staff is a tribute to the value placed upon their contributions to patient care. (Courtesy California Room, Feldheym Central Library.)

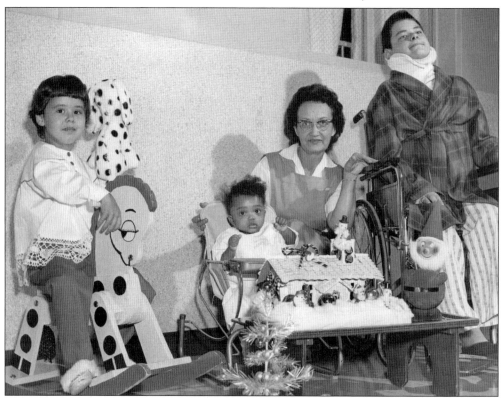

Bringing a little holiday cheer to the Orthopedic Ward is Nurse Ruth Barker. In the photograph from left to right are Jacqueline Valerie Paige riding the hobbyhorse, Mary Louise Gilbreth admiring the Christmas display, and Dale Owen in the wheelchair. The children attended the children's Christmas party at the Community Hospital. Santa Claus never forgot to visit the children's Christmas party, bringing gifts for each patient.

PINK IS BEAUTIFUL:

Such a busy, busy group is our Auxiliary! Once again Community reaped the benefits of the Pinks' sowing . . . the annual gift was $21,375.00 this year!! This was presented to Mrs. Henderson at the Annual Auxiliary Luncheon which is the Hospital's yearly way of saying "thank you."

Other recent activities included a new member coffee at which time Martha Fontaine, R.N., performed her first official duties as the new Auxiliary Director. Teddy Weeks, R.N., has resigned to take life easy and have a little fun.

Mrs. Henderson gratefully accepts Pinks' annual donation.

Martha Fontaine bids Teddy Weeks a Bon Voyage...

Smiling new comers join the Pinks...

Candy Striper demonstrates use of "their" gift Resusci Baby.

Virginia Henderson, Community Hospital administrator, wrote this article about the hard work of the auxiliary, affectionately known as the Pink Ladies. The article urges everyone to turn off lights in unused rooms, and reminded everyone that a hospital run efficiently saves money for every citizen. The auxiliary was an important part of this effort with all their fund-raising events, a role in which they still take great pride. (Courtesy California Room, Feldheym Central Library.)

Potential auxiliary members gather in their finest attire before the Annual Membership Luncheon hosted by the auxiliary on April 9, 1960. Hundreds of volunteers worked on behalf of the hospital to ensure its smooth operation and to raise needed funds. The auxiliary had three guiding principles: public relations, fund-raising, and service to patients.

Wearing fancy hats and dressing up were par for the course when attending the Membership Luncheon hosted by the auxiliary at their second annual event in 1960. This was an important first step in becoming a member of the organization. Stay-at-home moms found time to volunteer, meeting the needs of Community Hospital. During the three-day open house in April 1958, auxiliary members acted as tour guides for about 8,000 visitors.

Virginia Henderson (left) always supported the auxiliary. At the Annual Membership Luncheon, she and two other members find a quiet corner to catch up and make plans to make the next year even more successful. The auxiliary members filled every gap at the hospital, comforting the smallest of patients to raising thousands of dollars annually to buy equipment needed to run the state-of-the-art hospital.

Virginia Martin, president of the auxiliary (left), and hospital administrator Virginia Henderson (right) meet with an unidentified woman to plan the year's activities for the group. The women of the auxiliary took great pride in the work they did for Community Hospital, and it showed. "Our work has just begun," says Martin.

Auxiliary member Elise Baker brings a decorated tray to patients who had to be in Community Hospital over the holidays. Mrs. Richard H. Gwartney, another auxiliary member, made the decorations. In its first 10 years of service, the auxiliary logged over 200,000 hours of service to Community Hospital. Baker was the wife of Neal Baker, founder of one of the first fast-food restaurants in San Bernardino.

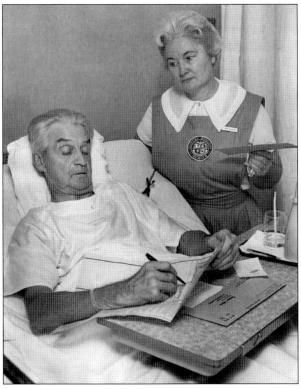

Making sure each vote counted was important. Here auxiliary member Mrs. John T. Schwab makes sure patient Marcus E. Shemars gets his chance to exercise his franchise in this November 8, 1960, photograph. The auxiliary originally organized in 1958, quickly grew from six to 39 members, and elected officers. The group was dedicated to Community Hospital, performing a variety of services over the years.

The auxiliary at Community Hospital helped celebrate many events over the years. An annual fund-raising dinner in the spring, a holiday party in December, and family outings for medical staff in the summer kept the auxiliary hopping. They organized teas, elected officers, trained new volunteers, and provided hundreds of thousands of hours of service in their first 10 years. These photographs are from March 1959.

Lab staff member Irene Dorner designed and made this sign for the Christmas party hosted by the auxiliary in 1960. The auxiliary organized the party, chose the delicious food and drinks, and decorated the rooms to make this annual event a special holiday treat for all dedicated staff members.

The auxiliary held a Christmas in November each year to raise funds and to make it easier for employees to shop during the holidays. This annual event raised many dollars with handmade gifts donated by members of the group. This is just one of the many events held during the season. Pictured from left to right are Mrs. Victor Gamber, Dr. Herman Bernstein, and nurse Ida Nielsen in 1960.

Being in the hospital during the holidays is never easy for the patient or the families of patients. Each year, the auxiliary worked tirelessly to make Community Hospital a more inviting place for all. Here two volunteers take a break from their activities, chat over coffee, and make plans for the New Year during the Christmas in November sale.

But it's only July! Preparing for Christmas in November always began early for the auxiliary. In July 1968, volunteers, from left to right, Mrs. Thomas Walton, Mrs. G. Wesley Davidson, and Virginia Martin (president) work tirelessly, tying ribbons on Christmas card holders they are making for the big sale.

Each year, the auxiliary created an annual cookbook by collecting favorite recipes from medical staff, administrators, and volunteers. The 1961 edition included "So Many Tasty Christmas Treats" that nurse Ada Lee Heckert (left) and volunteer Mrs. E. L. Fleming (right) just could not decide which one was the best. The recipes all look so delicious.

The holidays are an especially difficult time to be hospitalized, but each Christmas season, volunteers made sure that each patient received a bit of holiday cheer. Auxiliary member Ann Johnson (left) and Mrs. Edward Strum (right) ready the traveling punch bowl for its rounds of the hospital wings.

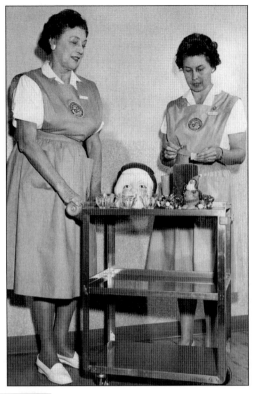

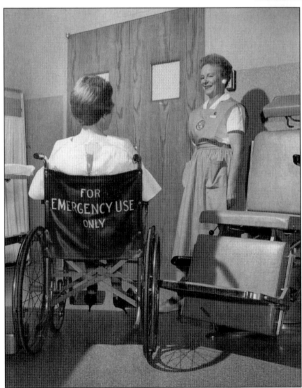

The auxiliary did more than just fund-raising at Community Hospital. Patient orientation and services were a part of their duties. Wheelchair tours were a specialty, and gave patients a clear understanding of the total operations of Community Hospital. Here Mrs. E. L. Fleming takes a patient on a tour that began in the emergency room.

51

An energetic group of young women formed a service organization called Candy Stripers. Each young woman was matched up with a member of the auxiliary who acted as the young woman's sponsor. Sponsors trained Candy Stripers to be proficient in the tasks they undertook, including delivering messages and tending the reception desk. The Candy Stripers are, from left to right, Stephanie Louison, Georgann Kirkpatrick, Pam Norfleet, Kathy Hill, and Jeanette Carter.

In 1968, some 20 employees could remember the move from the old building at Fourth Street and Arrowhead Avenue. A. P. Hinkleman, fondly referred to as "Hink," came to work in the X-ray lab of the old hospital in December 1945. Hink was a gifted X-ray technician who could get clear X-rays even under adverse conditions. Uncooperative patients or babies posed no challenge. Hink did it and did it superbly well.

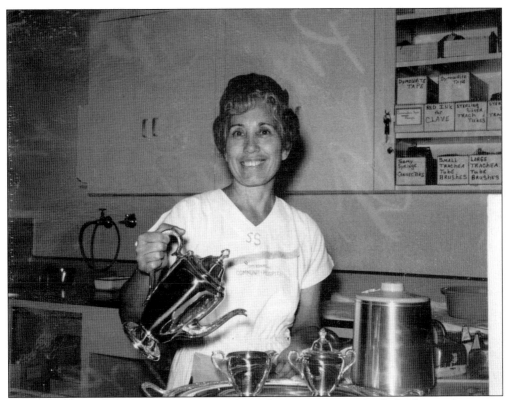

Door prizes from the annual Christmas in November event to raise funds for the auxiliary were something to look forward to all year long. Pictured is Dora Rodriquez from Central Supply, who won this tea service in 1965. The Christmas in November event was part holiday party and part bazaar, with many homemade gifts for sale to hospital employees.

The engineering department at Community Hospital had to accommodate a variety of requests, be flexible, and above all else be capable. They kept important systems humming. Louis Mayberry, pictured here in 1974, began as a trainee at Community Hospital in 1969 and quickly rose to licensed steam engineer by 1974. Louis had a friendly smile, and the staff was always pleased to see Lou respond when the hospital operator paged, "Engineer Stat!"

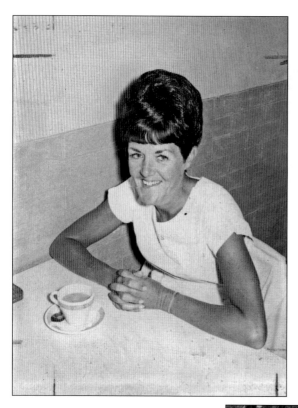

The operating room supervisor, registered nurse Sandra Hesterly, shown here, organized a statewide workshop for operating nurses in 1964. Hesterly served as the moderator for the event, which had speakers on the subjects of hyperpyrexia, afibrinogenemia, and cardiac arrhythmias among other subjects. This workshop was held at Community Hospital as part of its public service policy to provide continuing education for its staff.

Everyone at Community Hospital is important in making it as successful as it has been for 100 years, from world-renowned doctors to the housekeeping staff. Pictured is Larry Whitehead from housekeeping, reminding everyone that trash belongs in the litter bin and not on the ground. Community Hospital takes great pride in its campus and does its best to be a good neighbor in the surrounding areas.

In 1988, assistant director of Community Hospital Personnel, now known as human resources, was Deborah Lindsey. Meeting with employees, managers, and supervisors and explaining benefits, plus taking care of 100 different details, were all part of a day's work for Lindsey. The personnel department was a busy department as Community Hospital continued to grow.

No one dared challenge the wisdom of Charlotte Cottle regarding payroll and time and attendance records. A long-term member of the Community Hospital team, Charlotte did whatever it took to get the job done; that included educating employees on proper procedures. The fact that Community Hospital has a two-person payroll department that manages payments for more than 1,300 employees is testament to Charlotte's expertise. Charlotte joined Community Hospital in 1975.

"Just what I always wanted," said security guard Ray Farmer when he claimed his prize of automatic curlers during the holiday bazaar. Safety and security have always been important to Community Hospital staff. Security guards not only watched over the hospital but kept a watchful eye over the neighborhood as well. Farmer went on to be a distinguished local citizen.

John Gaygay, Community Hospital's head chef, could do things with food that made the average homemaker envious. He cooked turkeys quite a bit, especially for the employees' Christmas party in December. Everything was made on-site, including the baking of all bread and pastries. Large commercial ovens and a thoroughly modern kitchen made this possible when the new hospital was completed in 1958.

Chaplain David Randolph joined Community Hospital in 1974, moving from Santa Ana to San Bernardino. Chaplain Randolph worked part-time until he and his family completed their move from Santa Ana. Members of the hospital's spiritual care department are an important part of the health care team, making daily rounds and providing spiritual support 24 hours a day for patients, family, and staff who request it.

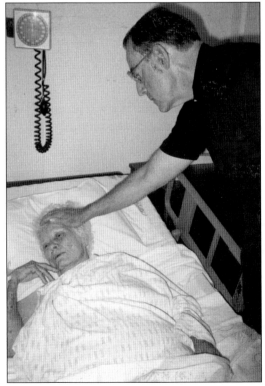

Recognizing and valuing a diversity of faith perspectives, Community Hospital's mission and core values have consistently embraced spirituality as part of a comprehensive approach to patient care. Upon admission, patients are asked if they would like to be visited by a hospital chaplain or a representative from their personal faith.

Clyde E. Coe was appointed executive housekeeper in 1972. Before accepting the position at Community Hospital, Coe served in the same position at Riverside Community Hospital and at the Mission Inn for 11 years. He was a past president of the Inland Executive Housekeepers Association. Clyde was well known for his meticulous attention to detail. Thanks to Clyde Coe, Community Hospital was always spotless.

Rosemary Caird, Queen of the Bay of Plenty Orange Festival at Tauranga, New Zealand, took time off from her duties at the National Orange Show to tour Community Hospital in 1973. As a medical technologist, Caird was interested in the equipment and layout of the lab at Community Hospital. Here Drs. Clark Forbes (left) and Charles Harmeling (right) show her through the modern facilities at Community Hospital.

Clara "Sally" Sallee, pictured here, came to work at Community Hospital in 1961 as an accounts clerk. By 1973, she was the jack-of-all-trades in the business office, assisting with posting, accounts payable, sorting of ledgers following posting, patient refund credits, and blood bank credits. She was never idle. Long before electronic record keeping, in a routine month, the business office's 38 employees handled 125,000 pieces of paper.

The hospital built in 1958 greatly expanded services for the San Bernardino community. During the 1960s, additions expanded those services even more. An expansion in 1967 allowed for improved facilities for organizing medical records. The medical records staff organizes and retrieves records quickly and efficiently. This made for swift access to vital information, necessary for the excellent level of care that residents had come to rely on at Community Hospital.

Clara Kay was one of 20 employees in 1968 that could remember the old hospital at Fourth Street and Arrowhead Avenue. Clara joined the staff as an aide in 1946. By 1968, Clara was working in pediatrics, also known as Wing 600. Virginia Henderson, hospital administrator, honored Clara for her 20-plus years of service to Community Hospital.

Nurse Irene McQueery was a veteran of the old downtown hospital as well, joining the staff in 1951. With 17 years of service under her belt, Irene embodies the commitment many Community Hospital employees have demonstrated. It was the family-like environment that kept many of the staff loyal to Community Hospital over the years.

Dorothy Payne, formerly of ICU, assumed direction of the emergency functions on the 7:00 a.m. to 3:00 p.m. shift. Payne had special training in intensive care and with the acutely ill or injured. Many nurses at Community Hospital were trained at the highly respected nurses training program at San Bernardino Valley Junior College. In-service training and continuing education events were common practice so patient care remained at superior levels.

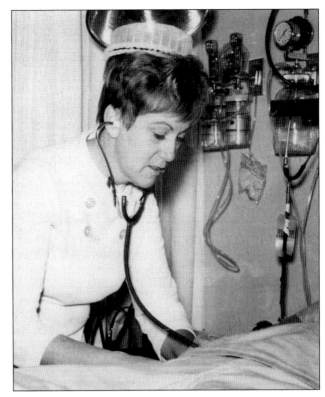

Beth Ford accepted the position of director of nursing in 1972. Ford came to Community Hospital after compiling a distinguished career at Morningside Hospital in Los Angeles, Tamalpais Hospital in Marin County, and Callison Memorial Hospital in San Francisco. Ford was a member of the California Nursing Association. Ford accepted the position because she was extremely impressed with the quality of nursing service at Community Hospital.

Marion Harris, RN, became the director of nursing at Community Hospital in 1978. A director of nursing (DON) is responsible for the standard of nursing practice in the hospital, supervising registered nurses and other staff members in providing comprehensive quality patient care. The DON establishes effective working relationships with the medical staff to ensure the medical plan of care is carried out.

Community Hospital has always provided an environment for professional development. Jan Vary, pictured here (center), began her career as a nurse's aide and has held a variety of nursing leadership positions over the years. In 2008, Jan was honored as Community Hospital's "Volunteer in Action" recipient. Today Jan heads up the orientation program for new hires and continues to educate clinical staff.

NURSING SERVICE ANNOUNCEMENTS

Carol Walsh, RN,
will do Infection Control

Jan Vary, RN,
ICU-CCU Supervisor

Gloria Clark, RN,
O.R.-P.A.R. Supervisor

The following supervisors will be helping shoulder the load here at Community:

Miss Jan Vary, R. N., no stranger to the physicians of Community, has accepted the position of ICU-CCU Supervisor. We are very pleased to have Jan since her long years of service here at Community uniquely qualify her for this position.

Mrs. Gloria Clark, R. N., has recently taken the position of O. R. and P. A. R. Supervisor. As we are all well aware, this is one of the most exacting positions in the nursing service. However, with Gloria's interest, enthusiasm, and expertise we are sure she will have a successful career.

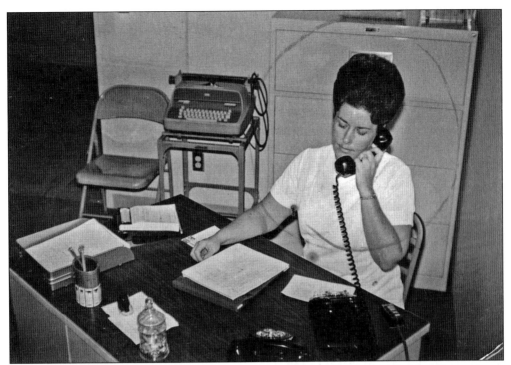

Joanne Raymer answers the phone for the Community Hospital's Nursing Service. No computer is in sight for this "gal Friday," but it's a sure bet she could get that typewriter flying. Nursing administration has evolved with new information technology and digital communication, but the supportive role in nursing administration is still essential.

Johanne Wise, RN (seen here), assistant to Ruth Barker, director of Nursing Service, institutes one of several measures to achieve closer contact between nurses, aides, and patients. Monthly conferences called together head nurses to gather suggestions for improving communication and to exchange ideas. Communications became the watchword for Community Hospital's nursing service in 1968.

In-service director Pat Herres, RN, ensured continuing education for the nursing staff. Maintaining current clinical competence and expertise, developing new skills, and maintaining CPR certification were important responsibilities of the education department. One of Herres's innovative programs was transporting pediatric patients via wagons—much less scary than a gurney or wheelchair.

Among the hospital employees who won prizes at the auxiliary's annual Christmas in November in 1970 was Janice McPhate (left), a director of the clinical laboratory for many years, who won a set of wall ornaments. Jan was instrumental in introducing technology, was meticulous in maintaining accreditation and compliance, and worked closely with the medical staff.

Two young members of the Ticktockers of National Charity League bring some of their decorated funny and fancy Easter eggs to Ruth Barker, supervisor of Nursing Service, for the shut-ins of the community. For years, the organization had the Easter project as one of their philanthropic projects. Pictured here are Cheri Crane (left) and Cathy Currie (right).

Dr. Frank Letson, an emergency room doctor at Community Hospital for many years, enjoys a rare quiet moment in a very busy emergency room. The number of cases seen in the ER daily almost doubled in the 1980s, but excellent patient care was always the first priority. Dr. Letson was known for his care and compassion in the community and was highly regarded for his leadership skills.

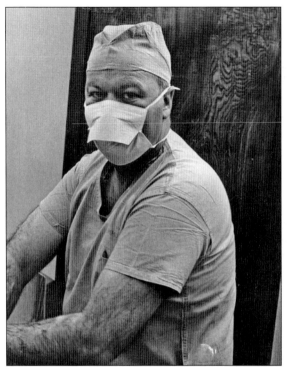

The staff surgeons at Community Hospital performed numerous surgical procedures. It was important to the hospital to continue to provide the latest technology. A Laminar Flow Ventilation system was installed in 1978, designed to reduce the possibility of infection. Pictured here is Dr. Wendell Mosley preparing for surgery.

Along with state-of-the-art operating rooms and excellent surgeons, anesthesiologists are key members of the surgical team. The anesthesiologist supports the surgeon by keeping the patient asleep, relaxed, safe, and stable. While delivering anesthesia, the anesthesiologist uses sophisticated monitoring equipment. In this photograph, Dr. Charlie Carmack administers general anesthesia to a surgical patient.

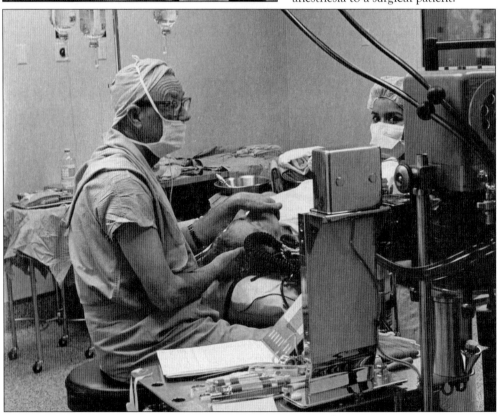

Dr. Ralph Mallinger (left) and Dr. Brian Eliker, both family medicine practitioners, cut up in the doctors' lounge. Dr. Eliker became associated with Community Hospital in 1956. He began by covering the emergency room and liked it. He said, "I would talk a patient into coming to Community down at Fourth and Arrowhead. . . . they were so pleased with the care . . . they had a reason to come to the hospital again."

Dr. Brian Eliker (left) and Dr. Max Goldstein reminisce about the "good old days." Dr. Goldstein joined the staff at Community Hospital right after World War II. He remembered the obstetrics department at the old Community Hospital: "The second floor was baby. [The room was] about three feet in diameter, one hundred and five degrees in the shade, [when] the window was open . . . you could look into the Justice Department of the courthouse."

Doctors met socially each year to catch up and take a break from their busy schedules. In this photograph, perhaps Dr. Rudy Hack (right), an obstetrician, is discussing the latest techniques in childbirth, or maybe he is saying how astounded he is by the increasing number of newborns at Community Hospital.

Obstetricians and family physicians do socialize. Here Dr. John Miller (left) and Dr. LeMon Smith (center), both obstetricians, laugh at one of Dr. Brian Eliker's (right) infamous jokes. Dr. Eliker remembered the "doctors had such a pleasant situation. There was no backbiting and by the time I finished my residency there was no question about where I wanted to go." Looks like Drs. Miller and Smith agree.

Dr. Joel Adams (left), an orthopedic surgeon, and Jim Regan (right), a physical therapist, have much in common. Five orthopedic surgeons practiced in San Bernardino in the 1970s: Drs. Joel Adams, Sean McAllister, Roger Dugan, Ben Houglin, and Robert Ballard. Community Hospital was at the cutting edge of the new hip replacement surgery that was being developed during this time.

Dr. Stanley Bishop, pictured here, served as president of Community Hospital's board of directors in 1980 when the board announced its intention to build a new 294-bed facility in Rialto. San Bernardino's city council formally opposed the move, but Bishop said the Rialto location was "clearly the best site" because a Westside expansion plan meant homeowners residing north of the hospital would have to be relocated.

Community Hospital pharmacists have earned and enjoyed the friendship and respect of the medical staff over the years. Pictured here are longtime director of the pharmacy Joe Neuman (left) and Dr. Daniel Gorenberg. Joe was known for his dedication, collaborative leadership style, clinical expertise, and ability to have fun. When he wasn't traveling to Latin American countries with his wife, he was known for working hard and playing hard.

Dr. George Small (left) was a very busy obstetrician at Community Hospital. Babies have always been special at Community. Prospective parents are invited to attend a Maternity Tea and Tour, which includes a complementary dinner and a tour of the private labor, delivery, and recovery suites. Family visiting hours are flexible, and fathers-to-be are welcome to stay overnight.

Dr. Alvaro Bolivar (left), a surgeon, anesthesiologist Dr. Catherine Rice (center), and surgical nurse Pauline Fernandez take a break from their busy day to enjoy dinner courtesy of the auxiliary in 1988. Pauline Fernandez began working at Community Hospital in February 1974. Fernandez says she has remained at the hospital because "this is like a family. . . . everyone supports everybody. . . . that's probably why I have been here so long."

Dr. Samuel Bolivar (left) and Dr. David Bolivar (right), along with their brother Alvaro, really did give Community Hospital a family atmosphere. Samuel practiced internal medicine while his brother David was in emergency medicine. All brothers were highly respected at Community Hospital, and their sense of humor made Community an easy, comfortable place to work. Here they are pictured enjoying dinner at Community Hospital in 1988.

The doctors at Community Hospital were routinely honored for their dedication to the hospital and the San Bernardino community. Here, from left to right, Drs. John Kohut, Ross Ballard, Alvin Russo, and Robert Ballard put the latest honor on display. Dr. Russo was president of the medical staff, became the chairman of the board of the hospital, and later served as medical director for about two years until he retired.

Dr. George Spelman, pictured here in 1980, began working at Community Hospital in 1948. Dr. Spelman, a graduate of Syracuse University, was one of a group of young doctors who wanted to gain accreditation for the hospital. He remembered this movement began in 1953, and gradually the members of the medical staff worked together so that by the end of 1955 they saw progress toward accreditation being made.

Socializing within the medical staff is an important part of the culture at Community Hospital. Pictured here are the members of the OFC in 1987. This group of retirees represents a very collegial, supportive cross-section of all disciplines of the medical staff. Their positive regard for each other and the hospital was evident.

Director of Medical Staff Services Diana Santini (center) and Dr. Talal R. Muhtaseb (left) honor Dr. Chittivelu Seshaiah. A specialist in infectious disease, Dr. Seshaiah was a warm and caring physician who found a special place in his heart for Community Hospital. His clinical and teaching skills and his soothing bedside manner were widely admired. Dr. Seshaiah spent many hours in the medical library, which was named for him after his death.

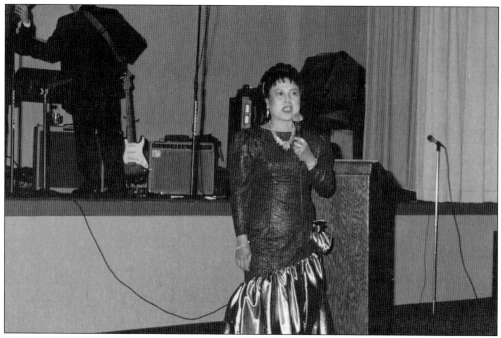

One of the traditions of the medical staff was to enjoy an annual holiday party they called Evergreen. This was a time to socialize and honor the leadership of the medical staff. Several of Community Hospital's physicians have more than medical skills; they bring their musical talent to the events as well. In this photograph, Dr. Godofreda Sumalangcay mesmerizes the audience.

Pictured here enjoying the medical staff Christmas party is Dr. Jason Lin. A pulmonologist and active member of the Community Hospital medical staff, Dr. Lin was known for his low-key, quiet personality and served as medical director of cardiopulmonary services for many years.

Ed Sorenson served as chief financial officer at Community Hospital for over 20 years. He is well respected in his field for his extensive knowledge of hospital financial management and his impeccable balance sheets. He is pictured here at the Evergreen Medical Staff Christmas Party in 1992 along with his lovely wife, Bonnie.

"No, don't take my picture!" says Stan Chrzan. But Stan is important to everyone at Community Hospital. Without him, nothing would work. Stan served as vice president of support services overseeing the efficient operation of Community's facilities for many years. Here he is seen enjoying a night off at the Evergreen Medical Staff Christmas Party in 1992.

Dr. Frank Letson and his wife, Linda, pose for the camera at the medical staff Christmas party in 1992. The Letsons continued the family atmosphere at Community Hospital. Dr. Letson practiced emergency medicine. Linda began as a nurse, and her career path led her to become chief operating officer at Community Hospital for many years. Both were highly respected and participated in many fund-raising activities for the hospital.

Ballroom-style dancing was in evidence with the members of the medical staff and their spouses along with the senior leadership team. Everyone looked forward to this annual event. It provided an opportunity for retired doctors to remain engaged with the current medical staff. This event was held in the Renaissance Room of the National Orange Show in 1992.

Four

OUR SERVICES

Once in its new facility, the hospital thrived. What followed in the 1960s and 1970s was a continuing program of expansion and modernization. By 1969, Community Hospital added a new 125-bed extended-care facility, a physical therapy building, an expanded maternity wing, and intensive and coronary care units. By 1971, extended-care beds were converted to acute care, and the licensed bed capacity increased to 322.

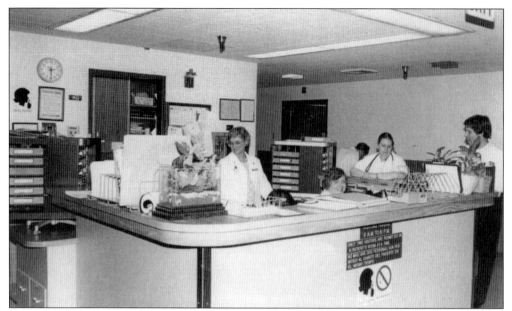

The nurse's station in the new hospital made patient care much easier. A centralized nurse's station with rooms just steps away enabled the nursing staff to care for patients more efficiently. At the old Ramona Hospital, staff had to run up and down stairs to care for their patients. This completely modernized nurse's station, with records and equipment close at hand, and made all the difference.

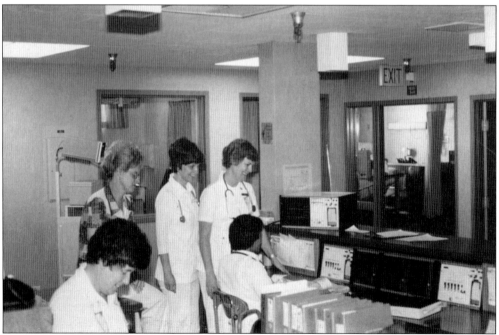

In 1967, Community Hospital converted a part of Wing 200 into the first CCU or coronary care unit. The CCU is a quiet, calm, and restful area where patients can be further evaluated and closely monitored. Specially trained nurses worked with doctors and other members of the medical team, providing specialized, individualized care.

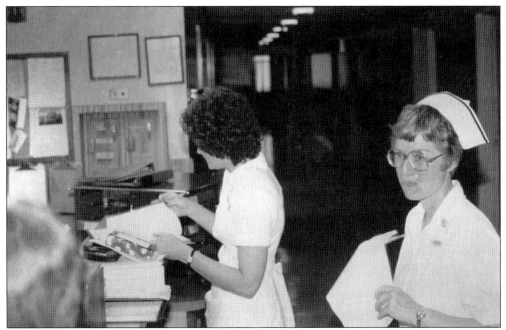

Nurses were always busy, and the nurse's station was the hub of all the activity. Wing 200 opened in 1962, adding new beds to the busy post-op floor. Three years later, another new wing was completed to house the clinical laboratory. Plans were always in the offing for any new additions that would improve patient care at Community Hospital.

This photograph of Wing 600, pediatrics, was taken in the early 1980s. The nursing staff, including student nurses and nurse's aides, played a vital part in the success of Community Hospital. Caring for ill and recovering children can be challenging, but they succeeded making it a bright and cheerful area that would appeal to children and their families.

Community Hospital delivers lots of babies. In 1958, columnist Earl Buie noted, "Within its very walls, an estimated 33,000 babies were born, more people than lived in the town during the first 20 years of the hospital's existence" at Ramona Hospital. The staff worked hard to make its maternity wing comfortable and inviting. In the 1970s, soft lighting, rocking chairs, and bedspreads made new moms and dads feel right at home.

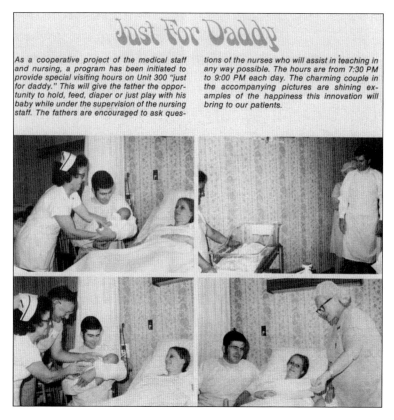

Just For Daddy

As a cooperative project of the medical staff and nursing, a program has been initiated to provide special visiting hours on Unit 300 "just for daddy." This will give the father the opportunity to hold, feed, diaper or just play with his baby while under the supervision of the nursing staff. The fathers are encouraged to ask questions of the nurses who will assist in teaching in any way possible. The hours are from 7:30 PM to 9:00 PM each day. The charming couple in the accompanying pictures are shining examples of the happiness this innovation will bring to our patients.

The obstetrics and delivery departments were continuously expanding during the 1960s and 1970s. This special area just for the fathers was a brand-new concept in 1973. Prior to this time, fathers were expected to wait outside of the delivery room. Community Hospital was well known over the years for its excellent maternal/child services. (Courtesy California Room, San Bernardino Public Library.)

The Ballard Rehabilitation Center, dedicated in 1985, was formerly Community Hospital Rehabilitation Center. The center had a therapeutic pool, a wheelchair-equipped van (donated by the auxiliary) for community outings, and a two fully equipped gyms to serve the needs of patients with diagnoses such as stroke, brain injury, spinal cord injury, amputations, post–hip surgery, and numerous other disabling illness and injuries.

Introducing fun into the rigorous rehabilitation program was always a goal of the center and would help patients return to a productive and fulfilling life. The Ballard rehab staff helped patients, often in wheelchairs, gain important physical and social skills, which enabled them to return to be productive members of the community. A high-energy volleyball game was played at the 1986 Rehabilitation Week celebration.

The Ballard Rehabilitation Hospital had a therapeutic pool and also included whirlpool baths and a fully equipped exercise gym for head and spinal cord injury patients. Small apartments allowed recovering patients to learn to cope with their everyday needs, maneuver wheelchairs, and prepare meals. Patients with orthopedic problems, stroke recovery, and neuromuscular disorders were all treated at Ballard.

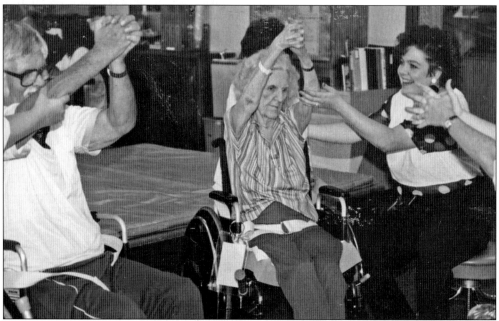

Occupational, physical, and speech therapists, rehabilitation nurses, and a physician specializing in rehabilitation medicine developed treatment plans that were carried out continuously during the inpatients' stay. During evening and night shifts, rehabilitation nurses supported daytime therapy activities. The focus of the program was to help patients to become as independent as possible and be discharged back to the community.

In 1972, Ballard Center was born out of the visions of its founders—nurse Mary M. Hunt (second from left), who continues as chief operating officer, and physical therapist James Ragan (far right)—who presented a proposal for a rehabilitation program to administrator Virginia Henderson (far left). Dr. Robert Ballard (second from right), an orthopedic surgeon, pioneered joint replacement surgery and was the center's first medical director.

Peggy Ann Moormeister (right) was the first "graduate" of Ballard Rehabilitation Hospital. Following an accident at age 17, Peggy spent 24 weeks in rehab. One year after her discharge, Peggy competed in the Special Olympics "Obstacle Course Event," beating the 10-year champion. Bill Sloan (left) suffered a stroke in 1993 but took away the attitude that a wheelchair couldn't keep him down. Bill completed law school after leaving Ballard.

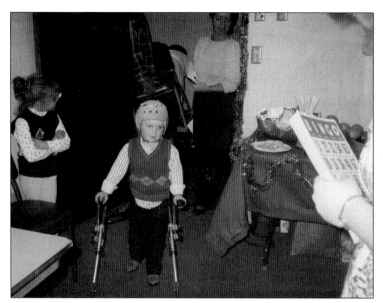

Ballard Center was certified by California Children's Services to care for pediatric patients. The center treated a young Afghani boy, pictured here, who lost both arms in a bomb explosion. He was fitted with bilateral prostheses, learned to use them well, and was returned to his country. Children are very resilient and capture the hearts of all who care for them.

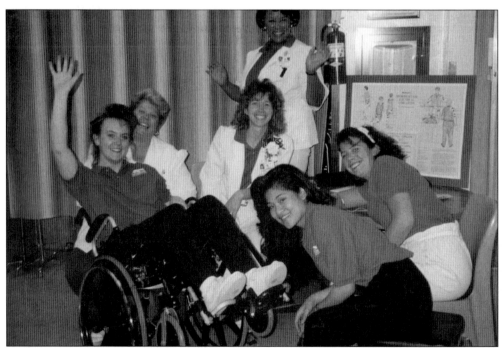

All work and no play makes Jack a dull boy . . . or so goes the philosophy of the Ballard staff. All kinds of crazy activities, such as wheelchair races, team games, and competitions, built morale and brought the team together. Ballard initiated the first rehabilitation technician program in the country; its therapists were highly trained, and many of Ballard's nurses were Certified Rehabilitation Registered Nurses.

Innovation has been integral to Community Hospital's culture over the years. The first private psychiatric inpatient facility in San Bernardino, called the Center for Mental Health, began in 1972 as an experimental program. It evolved into a regional mental health center, which included an adolescent psychiatric program, a state-certified, in-house school program for inpatients, and a comprehensive psychiatric unit.

The Adolescent Unit was a 24-bed program dedicated specifically to the treatment and assistance of youth ages 12 to 18 in the community who had alcohol and/or drug dependencies. The health of the entire family through individual, family, and group therapy was the focus of this unit. The unit had a fully accredited school and teachers to address the needs of the children and adolescents under its care.

This 23-bed unit offers psychiatric and dual-diagnosis inpatient treatment for adults 18 and older. The emphasis was on stabilizing and reintegrating the adult patient back into the community. The mental, social, emotional, and spiritual needs of the patient were closely monitored to ensure a smooth transition from the hospital back into the community.

In addition to the core inpatient programs, Community Hospital outpatient programs offered psychiatric evaluation and assessment. Comprehensive treatment was combined with referrals to appropriate caregivers and community-based services. Partial hospitalization and outpatient programs provided services for patients who did not meet the criteria for inpatient hospitalization but needed more than outpatient visits with a doctor or therapist. Pictured here is the entire Behavioral Health Services team.

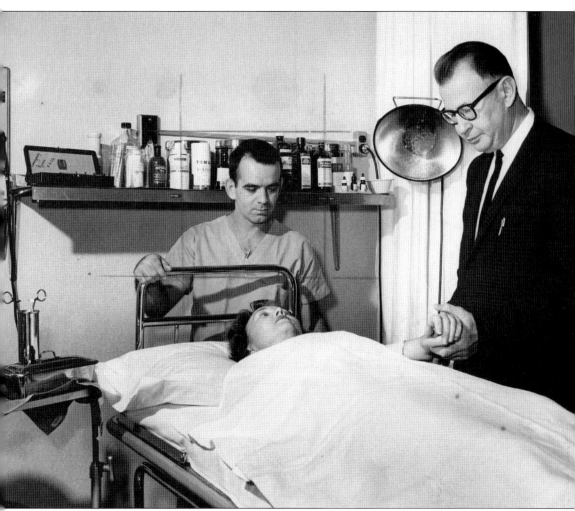

Here Dr. John McAlister (right), assisted by technician Jerry Dufour, examines their pretend accident victim, Mary Henry, in the Community Hospital Emergency Room. In 1964, San Bernardino physicians at Community Hospital and St. Bernardine's completed their first year of "round-the-clock" emergency services by a doctor. According to technician Jerry Dufour, the average daily patient load in the ER has jumped from 20, before 24-hour service began, to a current 35 to 40. Some weekends, he explained, have brought as many as 150 to the ER. Under the extended service, staff doctors take turns on ER duty, with a doctor on call during the day and in the hospital at night. (Courtesy California Room, Feldheym Central Library.)

Ora Oprandi makes the first call on the Hospital Emergency Administrative Radio (HEAR) installed in 1970 at Community Hospital, the base hospital for the Inland Empire network, which tied together 97 Southern California hospitals. This powerful radio system was able to operate in times of disaster even though telephone communication was disrupted.

This photograph is an early-1980s image of the emergency room at Community Hospital, which had an important place in the neighborhood and local area. Equipment and space needs evolved over the decades. Registered nurse Sandy Coleman joined Community Hospital in 1974 and continues to work as an emergency room nurse at Community Hospital today.

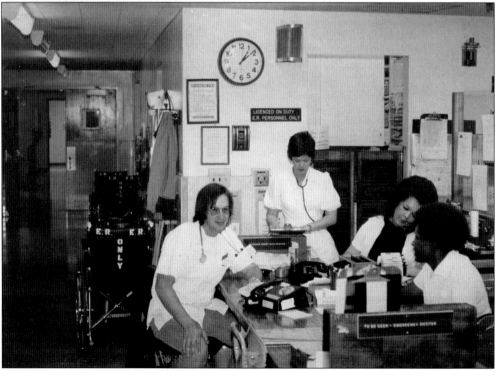

Community Home Health of San Bernardino opened in the mid-1980s and originally was known as the National in Home Health Care Agency. The program provided patients with the convenience of receiving clinical care in the comfort of their home with family members close by. Under the supervision of their doctor, registered nurses, home health aides, social workers, and physical, occupational, and speech therapists provided home visits.

In 1986, Community Hospital received a grant from the State Department of Aging to open a licensed Adult Day Health Care Center. Focused on the needs of frail, elderly patients, this program promoted the restoration and maintenance of physical and mental health, enhancing the quality of life and facilitating continued independent living in the community. Pictured here is Kimiko Ford (right) accepting the startup funding from the state.

In the 1990s, the program expanded to include an Alzheimer's Day Care/Resource Center. This program provided a safe and secure daily regimen for older adults suffering from Alzheimer's disease and related disorders. The family caregivers of these patients were able to enjoy four to six hours per day of respite from the demands of 24-hour care.

Funded in 1985 by a grant from the State Department of Behavioral Health, the Inland Caregiver Resource Center (ICRC) provided information, referral, and support to caregivers of brain-impaired adults. David Fraser (front left) directed ICRC, which assisted family caregivers who provided 24-hour care to loved ones with Alzheimer's, Parkinson's, and Huntington's diseases, stroke, or traumatic brain injury. In 1991, the ICRC became an independent nonprofit agency and continues to serve the community.

Working with doctors, a highly skilled clinical team in the Ambulatory Care Unit provided a wide range of services to patients of all ages. In addition to outpatient surgeries and endoscopic procedures, this unit provided blood transfusions, catheterization, wound care, IV antibiotics, chemotherapy, and pain management services to patients on an outpatient basis. Pre- and post-operative care was also available through ambulatory care.

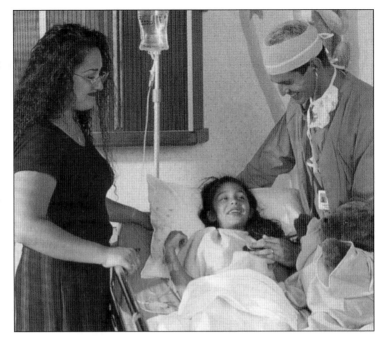

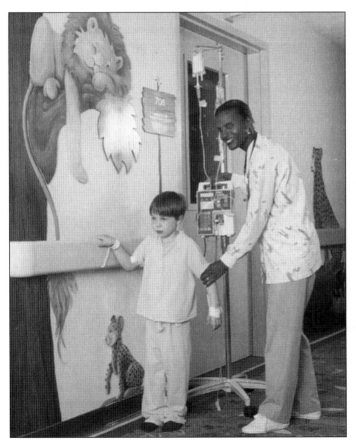

Specially trained clinical staff cared for children aged newborn to 16 in the pediatrics unit. Jungle animals lined the hallway, and a special "jungle" playroom stocked with toys provided a family-centered playful environment. This was part of everyday pediatric care at Community Hospital. To ease a child's anxiety, one parent was always welcome to spend the night.

Patients convalescing or in need of long-term skilled nursing were provided with all the services they needed to feel safe and comfortable in the 99-bed certified Community Convalescent Center. The clinical staff offered rehabilitation therapy, nursing care, dental services, and audiology and ophthalmology diagnosis and treatment. The fine dietary staff met each patient's unique needs, and a full-time activities director planned arts and crafts, games, and parties.

Activities Director Carol Howard checks the December calendar.

Executive Secretary Hope Jimenez and Admissions Coordinator Bill Shufran in the front office.

Pictured at left is activities director Carol Howard, who is checking the December patient activities calendar. On the right are executive secretary Hope Jimenez (center) and admission coordinator Bill Shufran in the front office. The center addresses more than the health needs of the residents. A typical monthly calendar includes coffee socials, pet therapy, music, and current events. Family members are invited to join the activities.

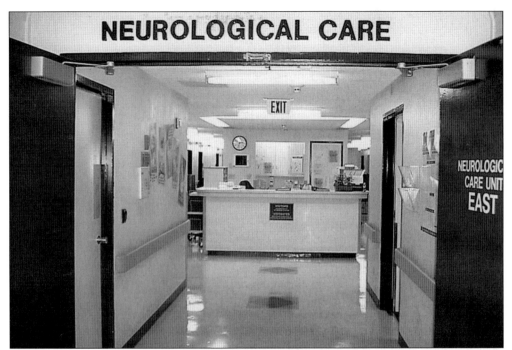

NEUROLOGICAL CARE

In 1993, a medical-surgical unit was converted into the first adult Neurological Care Unit (above). Subacute care is for patients who have stabilized from events such as congenital disorders, acute illnesses, or traumatic accidents and head injuries. Trachs, ventilators, and G-tubes are common medical necessities for many of these patients. A compassionate clinical staff with specialized skills and knowledge works hard to create a homelike environment to meet the needs of the patients. In 2004, the Community Convalescent Center (below) was converted into a specialized, 34-bed, freestanding Children's Subacute Center. Visitors cannot help but notice the bright frolicking sea creatures painted along the hallways. The caring and loving staff works around the clock to help each child attain a quality of life that allows them to reach their highest potential. The Children's Subacute Center puts each child first to help them achieve their recovery goal. At the Children's Subacute Center, smiles are contagious.

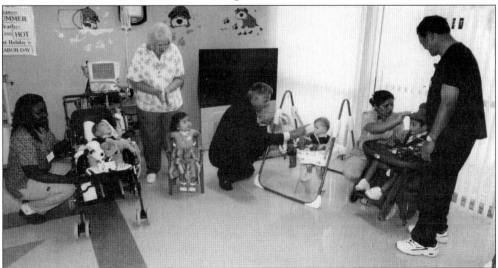

The Auto Analyzer was one of the most valuable contributions to laboratory science in 1968. This machine measured blood sample tubes in a revolving rack and could do as many as 12 different tests on one sample of blood. In this photograph, laboratory technologist Paul Watson is demonstrating the new equipment. An addition to the unit was a computer that records the results on graphs. Currently the clinical laboratory processes over 800,000 tests per year.

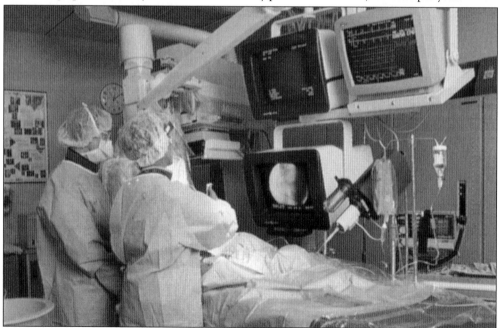

State-of-the-art equipment was available thanks to the auxiliary's primary goal—to raise money to support the Community Hospital and to stay current with advances in technology. The diagnostic radiology staff worked tirelessly 24 hours a day, seven days a week to meet the demands of a busy emergency department, acute care patients, and demanding outpatient schedule.

Pharmacists prepared medications in individual packages that allowed the nursing and medical staff to quickly and accurately identify medications. The experienced clinical pharmacists at Community Hospital were an integral part of the hospital's medical team and provided drug regimen reviews, drug monitoring, and education to Community Hospital's patients, staff, and doctors.

At Community Hospital, respiratory care practitioners, cardiac diagnosticians, nurses, EEG technicians, and ultrasound technologists performed a variety of procedures and tests in the Cardiopulmonary Services Department. Inpatient and outpatient services provided by this highly skilled clinical team were respiratory therapy, pulmonary function tests, EEGs, EKGs, and cardiac rehabilitation therapy.

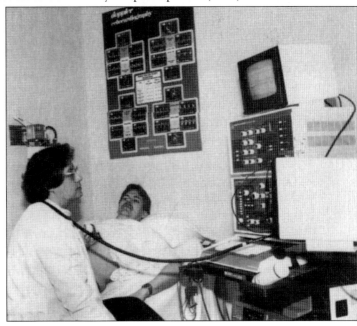

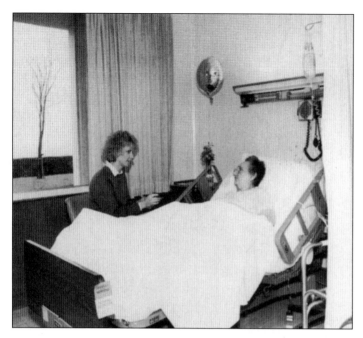

Pictured here is a hospital social worker helping a patient sort through her plans for services that will be needed when she is discharged from the hospital. Social workers were skilled at assessing the psychosocial needs of patients, facilitating communication with families and staff, and ensuring a coordinated plan of care was carried out.

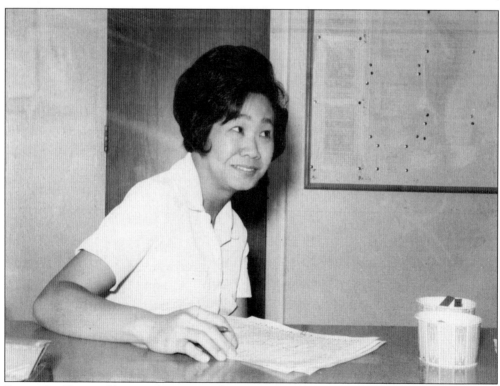

Pictured is Donna Ching, a therapeutic dietician who ensured that each patient's meals were healthful and met their needs. Before joining Community Hospital, Ching worked at White Memorial Hospital in Los Angeles. She is a native of Hawaii, and her husband was a third-year medical student at Loma Linda Medical School.

Five

GROWTH AND CHANGE

This aerial view of Community Hospital visibly demonstrates the "turtle" spoke-and-wheel design of the original facility constructed in 1958, along with multiple additions, new wings, and ancillary and support services that were needed to handle the growth of the community over the years. Physicians and staff appreciated the ease in which they could move from unit to unit and care for patients in the design-award-winning facility.

A new five-story, 150,000-square-foot expansion to the hospital brought Community Hospital much needed space for more patient rooms, an emergency center, diagnostic imaging, a cardiopulmonary center, a much larger cafeteria, and a state-of-the-art intensive and coronary care unit. With the help of a very large gift from San Bernardino resident Monida Cummings, $2.3 million was raised from over 800 contributors.

Ground-breaking ceremonies for "The New San Bernardino Community Hospital" were held on November 20, 1986. Chairman of the hospital board Marvin M. Reiter (sixth from right), chairman of the nonprofit parent corporation Arrowhead Healthcare System Harold K. Hunt (eighth from right), and chief of the medical staff John P. Morris (seventh from left) join hospital CEO Ray H. Barton III (fourth from right), hospital board members, and local dignitaries for the celebration.

The new tower was designed to adapt to ground movements in the event of an earthquake. A 6-inch seismic joint runs through the entire building. This joint allows both sides of the building to move independently with a quake. With the new tower came greatly needed new technology for diagnostic purposes and to provide patient care monitoring and life support where needed.

The expansion of the hospital consisted of a five-story patient tower, adding 139 beds to the hospital. The new services included special labor, delivery, recovery, and postpartum beds and a completely equipped surgery so that caesarian section births could be performed in the maternity suite. Five neonatal intensive care unit beds complemented the new nursery. Four operating rooms, including a special cystoscopy room, were included in the new surgical department.

The topping-out ceremony was held June 2, 1987, for the new five-story, 150,000-square-foot tower addition to Community Hospital. This photograph was taken at that event, which also changed the name of the street that ran between the two sections of the hospital campus. The street had previously been known as Muscott Street and was renamed Medical Center Drive. The hospital's strong, positive impact on the city was one of the deciding factors in the state's and City of San Bernardino's approval of a $35-million, tax-exempt bond issue to support Community Hospital. Pictured above are, from left to right, Harold Hunt, Marvin Reiter, Dan Frazier, Valerie Pope-Ludham, Evlyn Wilcox (mayor of San Bernardino), and hospital CEO Ray H. Barton III.

Monida Browning Cummings, pictured at right, was born in Ogden, Utah, in June 1892, one of 10 children of John Moses and Rachel Child Browning. She married Nephi W. Cummings, a physics professor at San Bernardino Valley College. Monida Cummings's father designed and fashioned a breech mechanism for rifles and was referred to as "The Father of Modern Firearms." At the age of 24, he was issued his first U.S. patent on the Winchester rifle but allowed Winchester, Colt, and Remington to use their names on firearms made under his patent.

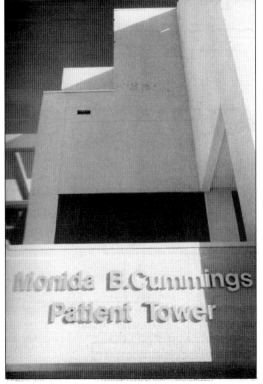

Monida Cummings, a longtime supporter of Community Hospital, contributed $1 million to build the new patient tower that greatly expanded services. The new building was named the Monida B. Cummings Patient Tower to honor her gift.

Community Health Systems of San Bernardino

Creating and providing health care solutions for our community

In the 1980s, with Ray H. Barton III leading the organization, Community Hospital diversified its programs to meet the needs of the community. On October 22, 1985, the hospital board and the 150-member community corporate board established a new parent organization known as the Arrowhead Healthcare System. Under the auspices of the new corporate structure, a continuum of services was developed or acquired, including a 99-bed skilled nursing facility, a licensed home health agency and adult day health program, a durable medical equipment company, a regional mental health program, special programs for seniors, and more. Under the leadership of the new CEO, Bruce Satzger, on May 2, 1995, the parent company's name was changed to "Community Health Systems of San Bernardino, Inc." CHS continued to be governed by a community corporate board consisting of 150 individual members who were residents, business owners, and physicians in the area served by Community Hospital until 1998.

By the early 1990s, Community Hospital's board had determined that aligning with a larger system, which would have the necessary resources to weather difficult financial times, would strengthen the hospital's future. The board evaluated a number of options and identified Catholic Healthcare West (CHW) as the hospital system that most closely aligned with its mission and values. On August 14, 1998, Community Hospital joined CHW. Above are representatives from CHW honoring the nursing and ancillary leaders of Community Hospital and St. Bernardine Medical Center (now a sister facility) for their collaborative work in 2000. At right is a snapshot of CHW's system president, Lloyd Dean (left), visiting Community Hospital. Enjoying the moment is Willi Shans, currently the longest serving employee with over 45 years of service. Willi's warm smile and hugs are still shared by employees and visitors.

Members of Community Hospital's Patient Satisfaction Steering Committee attend the CHW Quality Summit meeting on October 19, 2005. In keeping with the competitive spirit behind the CHW Lloyd Dean Challenge, the Community Hospital team came dressed in the official "Holy Mackerel" shirts. Home Health's Marnyce Jackson designed the logo, a mackerel with a halo. Community Hospital subsequently achieved a "Five Star Service" award from Avatar International, Inc., in 2006 for the improvement in patient satisfaction measures.

"Art that Heals" was the core theme of a project in 2008. The project included representatives from the hospital's broader faith community, using art, educational sessions, and dialogue to enhance an appreciation and sense of respect for the impact of diverse cultural and spiritual beliefs as a source of healing. Here, from left to right, are Rex Sia, Nenechi Anyakora, Mark Winick, Sandra McManus, and Terry Taylor viewing examples of Jewish art.

Six

OUR ADMINISTRATION

Dr. Henry William Mills was a first-class surgeon, a farsighted businessman, and an active member of the community. He was a member of the Phoenix Lodge 178, Keystone Chapter 56, San Bernardino Lodge 856 of the Benevolent and Protective Order of Elks, as well as several other groups. Dr. Mills can be credited for instituting a commitment to community service as well as excellent medical care at Community Hospital.

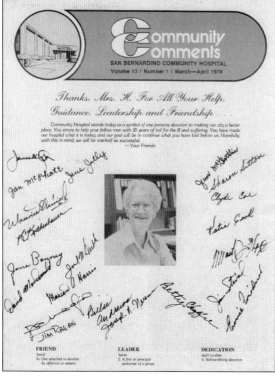

Community Comments
SAN BERNARDINO COMMUNITY HOSPITAL
Volume 13 / Number 1 / March—April 1978

Thanks, Mrs. H. For All Your Help,
Guidance, Leadership and Friendship . . .

Community Hospital stands today as a symbol of one persons devotion to making our city a better place. You strove to help your fellow man with 35 years of toil for the ill and suffering. You have made our hospital what it is today, and our goal will be to continue what you have laid before us. Hopefully, with this in mind, we will be one-half as successful.
— Your Friends

FRIEND | LEADER | DEDICATION

Perhaps no one served the interests of Community Hospital more strongly than Virginia Henderson. Beginning as an office manager in 1943 at the old Ramona Hospital, Henderson became one of the first women in the country to serve as a hospital administrator. Under her watchful administration, Community Hospital was accredited, built a new state-of-the-art facility, and ensured its smooth operation. In April 1978, Henderson retired as Community Hospital's administrator after 35 years of dedicated service to the hospital and the community. Her retirement party was a gala event attended by doctors, nurses, staff, political dignitaries, and community members.

Joel Deeble began at Community Hospital as hospital controller. In 1976, Virginia Henderson promoted Deeble to assistant administrator. In this position, Deeble dealt with a multitude of government regulations and a rapidly expanding hospital. After Henderson's retirement in 1978, Deeble became the administrator of Community Hospital, where he found himself dealing with trying to figure out how to pay for salary increases and mounting operating costs.

When Ray H. Barton III was brought on board as the CEO of Community Hospital following Joel Deeble's tenure, the financial challenges were increasing. Under Barton's direction, the hospital embarked on a "turn-around" and diversification program, positioning itself to sustain the core business of acute medical-surgical services and the growing rehabilitation and mental health service lines. Pictured here is Barton gratefully accepting the auxiliary's annual donation from Betty Clark.

Robert S. Lund was Community Hospital's administrator/CEO during the Arrowhead Healthcare Systems era. While Ray H. Barton III oversaw Community Hospital's parent corporation, Bob focused on keeping Community Hospital on track. Bob was known for his down-to-earth collaborative leadership style. His warm smile and friendly embrace was characteristic, as shown here at a recognition program.

Charles "Charlie" E. Kraus (right) was the president and CEO of Arrowhead Healthcare Systems following Barton's departure in 1989. With a background in finance, he was known for carefully watching the hospital's fiscal resources. Pictured with him at the 1992 medical staff Christmas party was director of Strategic Planning Clifford R. Daniels (left) and obstetrician Dr. Talal Muhtaseb (center).

Dr. Stanley Bishop (right), then chairman of Community Hospital's Board of Directors, served briefly as the interim hospital administrator in 1994. Once again, the hospital was experiencing financial challenges. Ballard Rehabilitation became a freestanding facility in 1993. The hospital continued to diversify by planning for the first subacute service wing on the East Campus. Dr. Bishop later served as vice president of medical affairs for the hospital.

Bruce Satzger joined the hospital in 1994. In 2004, Community Hospital was named one of the best places to work among businesses with 1,000 or more employees. Satzger oversaw Community Hospital's decision to join with Catholic Healthcare West. With the agreement, Community Hospital retained self-governance, remained a separate, nonprofit subsidiary responsible for its own budget, and continued to meet the needs of the community.

Interim president Jeff Flocken (right) is shown here at Community Hospital's 2005 Employee Service Awards dinner. Under his leadership, Community Hospital continued to hit high marks for patient satisfaction and other performance measures. Jeff is pictured here with, from left to right, director of Perioperative Services Pauline Fernandez, board chair John Nolan, and service award honoree Judy Figueroa, RN. Judy was celebrating 35 years of service at Community Hospital.

In 1995, Bruce Satzger was able to convince Diane Nitta to join the senior management team as SVP Clinical Services/CNE. In 2006, Diane was tapped to serve in the role of hospital administrator/interim president. Diane's ability to mentor her directors and provide them with growth opportunities allowed the hospital to add key programs and thrive in a challenging economic market. She is pictured here at the auxiliary's 50th anniversary celebration.

Seven

LIVING OUR MISSION

The Focus 92411 Neighborhood Council was a collaborative partnership between Community Hospital, California State University San Bernardino, San Bernardino Public Health Department, and the community. The council focuses on prioritizing the needs of the 92411 Zip code area and developing programs aimed at improving the well-being of residents. Here Jamie Alvarez (right) receives the first Neighborhood Partnership Award from Beverly Earl for his work in cleaning up blighted areas and restoring community spirit.

Juanita Scott (right) and Felton Anderson (left) organized a tutoring program for children on the Westside through Focus 92411. College students and community members volunteered their time to ensure that children had supervision between the end of school, about 2:30 p.m., until their parents came home from work at about 5:00 p.m. In addition to tutoring on Saturday mornings, girls in the area met to talk about nutrition, health, and other topics of interest.

Hospital employees from the Pharmacy, Food Services, Home Health, Cardiopulmonary, Clinical Lab, Medical Imaging, Volunteer Services, and Human Resources spoke to over 300 students during Career Day at San Andreas High School. The speakers focused on achieving goals and careers in health care. In this photograph, Fernando Mondragon, supervisor/clinical coordinator of Clinical Laboratory, speaks to students about careers in laboratory sciences.

On December 3, 1996, Hall of Fame football hero Dick Butkus visited Community Hospital, where he signed autographs and visited with patients. Over the years, famous athletes gave freely of their time to put smiles on the faces of seriously ill children. These four little patients in the pediatric ward could not be happier unless, of course, they were going home.

For many years, Community Hospital provided health fairs, particularly focusing on the needs of children. More than 75 children were immunized during this event held on October 25, 1997. In this photograph, Scott Browar, vice president of Clinical Services, administers an immunization to a child while her mother looks on. The annual "Kid's Care Fair" immunized children who may otherwise not have received these necessary vaccines.

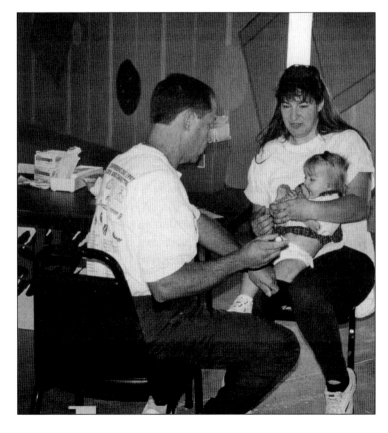

In 2001, Community Hospital was among eight organizations to receive Proposition 10 funding to expand access to services, expand the Babies First program, and develop educational program materials in plain language for the bilingual community. Pictured here from left to right are Frances Pagdilao, Linda McDonald, Drew Gagner, Susan Smith, Randy Hill, Roz Nolan, and Jerri Smith.

The Holiday Door Decorating contest was an annual tradition at Community Hospital. Departments compete to win prizes for the best decorated door. This event always adds to the festive holiday atmosphere at the hospital. Here, from left to right, auxiliary member Dick Bryant, principal of Inghram Elementary School Janie Morales, and Community Hospital's Chairman of the Board Frank Lyman judge this year's contest.

The Community Hospital Foundation's Annual Golf Classic was held to raise funds for Community Hospital. The women who oversaw the sign-up table in 1986 were led by Virginia Henderson (left). The foundation organized and ran many community-wide events, such as the Golf Classic, to bring friends and funds to support the hospital, a practice that continues today.

Ready to tee up, gentlemen? Don't worry about that handicap; it's all for charity anyway. The annual Community Hospital Foundation Golf Classic fund-raiser attracts all sorts of golf enthusiasts and raises funds for the newest hospital equipment and supplies. Over the years, the golf tournament has become known as one of the best in the region. The same can be said for the hospital it supports.

Community Hospital Foundation's Annual Golf Classic was known to be one of the best in the region. This was due in large part to the wonderful volunteers who took the time to ensure the golfers were well fed and had plenty to drink and the contests, raffles, and auctions were managed with efficiency. These volunteers managed to have fun while they supported a worthy cause.

The Golf Classic had a unique quality that other tournaments could not match—an outstanding team of executive chefs who could deliver lavish gourmet dinners at the event. Golfers, guests, and volunteers appreciated the creativity of the menus and beauty of the presentation. Pictured here seated is director of Food Services Ron Burton, surrounded by his team of fellow Sodexho and Community Hospital chefs.

It was easy to capture pictures of smiling golfers at the foundation's annual event. Who wouldn't enjoy a day of sunshine (there were only a few rainy days), great food, and a wonderful venue at the Arrowhead Country Club in San Bernardino? Pictured here is Community Hospital's clinical laboratory medical director, Dr. Robert J. Hubbard (left), along with senior director of Ancillary and Food Services Phil Liang.

Volunteers were essential for a smooth-running golf tournament. They were also greatly appreciated for pitching in and getting the job done. Much of the work was behind the scenes and required attention to details. In this photograph, manager of Volunteer Services Cindy Blackburn takes a break with manager of Plant Maintenance Rick Arnold. Arnold has 30 years of service with Community Hospital's Engineering Department.

By 2008, the Community Hospital's auxiliary had logged over one million hours of volunteer service and contributed over $1 million for the purchase of much needed equipment for the hospital. These achievements don't happen by accident. Volunteers like Donna Fischer (left) and Dottie Allison (right) were credited with providing the inspiration and leadership for others to follow. In this photograph, they are helping at a golf tournament.

The Ancillary and Support Services work hand-in-hand with nurses, physicians, and staff to ensure rapid turn-around times for high volumes of diagnostic tests and the provision of medications and nutritious food for patients and staff. They are responsible for the maintenance of facilities, the provision of human resources, marketing and communications, and spiritual support. This team contributed these services with a tremendous spirit of giving from the heart.

Betty Clark (left) served as a vice president of the auxiliary in 1979 and president from 1983 to 1985. Clark headed the auxiliary campaign to raise funds to build the Monida Cummings tower pledging to raise $200,000 over three years. Volunteers asked for pledges and held fund-raisers to meet their goal. In this photograph, Clark visits with auxiliary members selling handmade toys to meet the $200,000 goal.

Each year, Community Hospital hosted a "thank-you" event for auxiliary members. Rowena Pinckert, pictured here with her husband, Victor, in 1984, began volunteering at Community Hospital in 1965. Volunteers were very dedicated to the hospital. Rowena Pinckert remembered that the women came as volunteers but knew they were expected to be there when scheduled. They were there, or they found a substitute.

Community Hospital Auxiliary members take time out from their hundreds of duties to attend the Volunteer Recognition Luncheon. Each year, Community Hospital salutes its hardworking auxiliary members with a special event. Ida Mae Rolls (left), manager of Infection Control, and auxiliary member Dorothy Williams (right) enjoyed the festivities at the 2007 luncheon.

After serving in the Navy Medical Corps during World War II and working in the hospital pharmacy for many years, Madeline Hotch (left) joined the Auxiliary in 1969. As auxiliary president, Hotch made sure that the funds they raised bought a blanket warmer for the emergency room. Hotch is pictured here with Harold Newton, senior director of Pharmacy and Support Services at the 2007 Volunteer Recognition Luncheon.

The idea of forming an auxiliary was something Virginia Henderson envisioned in 1958. She approached the doctors and staff, suggesting that volunteers could benefit the hospital through public relations, fund-raising, and service to patients. Since the auxiliary's founding, it has contributed more than one million hours of service and raised money for equipment and supplies. Pictured here are the members of Community Hospital's auxiliary in 2008—50 and fabulous!

In 2008, Community Hospital honored the tireless devotion of the auxiliary by throwing a 50th anniversary bash. A 1950s theme with poodle skirts, bobby sox, and good old rock 'n' roll music ruled at the special luncheon held at the Orange Show. In this photograph, the senior director of Neuro/Behavioral Services/Public Safety, Larry Lawler, joins in the fun by playing the role of a "cool jerk."

Celebration is built into Community Hospital's culture of giving. Shown here having fun and making our day is the Public Safety/Communication Department's Loretta Robinson (left) and senior director of Clinical and Community Services Roz Nolan. Roz earned the San Bernardino County "Hospital Hero" award in 2008 for her leadership in achieving the UNICEF/WHO "Baby Friendly" designation for Community Hospital's Maternal/Child Care services unit.

Seen here are employees enjoying a tradition of annual employee service award celebrations. Hosting special events such as this luncheon were important to the hospital's leadership team to recognize the value of its employees. Holiday parties, luncheons, and dinners were held throughout the year to thank and support the staff of Community Hospital for their service and dedication to the hospital and community.

The Values in Action Awards were established by the Catholic Healthcare West Board of Directors to honor those who contributed to CHW's health care commitment in an exceptional way. Recipients were honored for their ability to infuse CHW's values into their lives, both on the job and in their community. This photograph above, taken in 2007, includes a group of past recipients, from left to right: Robert Redden, Information Services; Caroline Swinton, Patient Relations/ Risk Management; Hermo Malaguit, Medical Imaging; Yvette Whittaker, Care Management and Physician Support; Gloria Evans, Medical Imaging; and Cindie Fike, ICCU, ED, Telemetry, and Dialysis. Not pictured are Khadija Kelsick, Environmental Services, and Eloisa Lechuga, Maternal Child Health. Pictured below are Dr. Horace Stevens (second from left) and Dr. Debbie Bervel (second from right) receiving their award in the Emergency Department.

Nominee Sue Bawcum impressed her colleagues with her big heart and great sense of humor. No job was too big or too small for this team player. Always volunteering whenever she could help, her support was critical to the success of the Mission Integration team. Sue (center) is pictured here with board chairman John Nolan (left) and hospital administrator Diane Nitta (right) at the 2008 Values in Action luncheon.

Good food and conversation were a part of every event at Community Hospital. Values in Action was no exception. Pictured here are members of Community Hospital's housekeeping, food services, and neurocare services. Everyone joined in the celebration to honor those who contributed to Community Hospital's commitment to health care and community service.

Community Hospital serves the community by offering an annual walk-up or drive-thru flu shot clinic. Health care nurses screen each person before they receive their shot. In 2007, nearly 700 community residents received a free flu vaccination. More than 20 nurses along with pharmacy staff, EVS, Materials Management, Food Services, and the auxiliary volunteered their time to give residents easy access to preventive care.

Since 1974, the American Cancer Society has designated the third Thursday of November as the Great American Smoke Out, challenging smokers to stop using tobacco. According to the American Cancer Society, "In many towns and communities, local volunteers support quitters, publicize the event." At Community Hospital, the auxiliary participated in the event by sponsoring the "Adopt a Smoker" campaign to help smokers improve their health.

There are few moments in a professional career when success emerges despite what appear to be huge barriers. For the Community Hospital's medical staff and employees, the Joint Commission Survey score of "99" was that moment in October 1997. Pride is evident in the smiles of the

After two years of intense preparation, Community Hospital was designated as one of 61 "Baby Friendly" hospitals across the nation by the World Health Organization (WHO) and United Nations Children's Fund (UNICEF). To earn the designation, the hospital had to put 10 steps in place, including not accepting free or low-cost breast milk substitutes, not using bottles or pacifiers, practicing exclusive breast-feeding, "rooming-in" with parents, and feeding on demand.

Community Hospital team who worked together to reach this pinnacle of success. These individuals truly embodied the mission and values of Community Hospital.

Community Hospital partnered with San Bernardino Valley College to develop the Exclusive Nursing Program. With Community Hospital support, Valley College added 10 additional students to their training program each year. The students performed clinical rotations exclusively at Community Hospital. With this tuition reimbursement program, students committed to work at Community Hospital for three years after graduating. Supporting this new pipeline of nurses was a win-win for all.

Across America, People are Discovering Something Wonderful. Their Heritage.

Arcadia Publishing is the leading local history publisher in the United States. With more than 5,000 titles in print and hundreds of new titles released every year, Arcadia has extensive specialized experience chronicling the history of communities and celebrating America's hidden stories, bringing to life the people, places, and events from the past. To discover the history of other communities across the nation, please visit:

www.arcadiapublishing.com

Customized search tools allow you to find regional history books about the town where you grew up, the cities where your friends and family live, the town where your parents met, or even that retirement spot you've been dreaming about.